SANCTUARY

SANCTUARY

MARSHA CROCKETT

BETHANY HOUSE PUBLISHERS
MINNEAPOLIS, MINNESOTA 55438

Sanctuary: Finding Safe Places for a Woman's Soul
Copyright © 1999
Marsha Crockett

Cover illustration by Julia Lundman
Cover design by Eric Walljasper

Published by Bethany House Publishers
A Ministry of Bethany Fellowship International
11400 Hampshire Avenue South, Minneapolis, Minnesota 55438
www.bethanyhouse.com

Printed in the United States of America by
Bethany Press International, Minneapolis, Minnesota 55438

Library of Congress Cataloging-in-Publication Data

Crockett, Marsha, 1957–
    Sanctuary : finding safe places for a woman's soul / by Marsha Crockett.
      p. cm.
    ISBN 0-7642-2189-2
    1. Suffering—Religious aspects—Christianity. 2. Suffering in the Bible
Meditations. 3. Life change events—Religious aspects—Christianity.
4. Christian women Prayer-books and devotions English. I. Title.
BV4909.C76 1999
248.8'43—dc21
                                        99–6411
                                           CIP

To my husband, John,
who consistently creates
safe places within our lives
to grow together in Christ.

MARSHA CROCKETT has written two books, has been a contributor to three others, and has had numerous articles published in Christian magazines. A popular speaker/teacher, she creates a continual visibility for her books. She and her family make their home in Arizona.

For more information on her speaking and writing ministries, you may contact Marsha at:

671 North Stacie Court
Chandler, AZ 85226

(480) 961–4173

mkcrockett@aol.com

ACKNOWLEDGMENTS

Never in all my writing activity have I felt such a sense of team effort as on this project. I'm almost embarrassed to have my name alone as the author. So I'm happy to use this page to properly acknowledge those who have contributed so heavily to the development and writing of this book:

First, my family, both immediate and distant—especially my husband, John, and our daughters, Megan and Amy. They give me what every writer dreams of having—a cheering section of my own.

The six wonderful women of my Tuesday morning critique group—Betty Arthurs, Linda Carlblom, Marion Hocking, Andrea Huelsenbeck, Jane Jimenez, and Judy Robertson. Their ability to be gently brutal helped me through the day-to-day effort that writing requires.

The friends who prayed for me, read chapters, suggested ideas, and connected me to others who could help. Thanks especially to Dorothy Barnes, Barbara Milligan, Lisa Evjen, and Tricia Rhodes.

The wonderful team at Bethany House Publishers, especially my editor and friend, Steve Laube. He not only brought this project to fruition but has been a source of continual encouragement from my earliest writing days. He holds the standard high both professionally and spiritually and challenges me to stretch my writing wings.

Finally, the nine other women whose stories make up this book. They fearlessly opened their hearts, wept through interviews, and, at the same time, invited me to go deeper with them into the sanctuary of God. May God bless your obedience to him. I'm honored to call you my friends.

Contents

INTRODUCTION

I crouched low between the bush and the wooden fence. Splinters scraped the back of my bare arms. I heard his footsteps come closer and held my breath. He stopped in front of my hiding place but then walked on. I slowly let out my breath and waited ten, fifteen seconds more. Moving my head slightly to the right I peeked around the bushy branch. All clear.

I jumped into the open and ran as hard as I'd ever run to the porch swing. "Home free!" I yelled to my big brother, now on the other side of the house. Finally, I'd won. As he rounded the corner he asked, "Where were you?"

"I'm not telling," I smiled as I pumped my legs to the rhythm of the swing. "Now you hide." And we were off for another round of hide-and-seek.

That childhood game of hide-and-seek has become a symbol of my spiritual life. At times I make my own hiding places. I try to cover up my pain or sin or disappointment, like Adam and Eve hoped to cover their own nakedness from their Creator.

There is a moment in time when I must see that I'm not fooling anyone. I have to decide to move out into the open, to leave my self-made hideout, and to run to a place where I can call out, "I'm home free. . . ." That's the moment when I must choose to look to God and enter into his sanctuary or stay hidden in fear and live with the splinters and more serious heart-wounds of life.

No one has ever lived an entire life without experiencing fear. We're born with instinctive fears, in part as a survival mechanism. Even a newborn, if held a few inches above a bed and allowed to gently fall to a cushion, will instinctively spread out stiff arms and legs to keep from falling. They cry at loud noises. Toddlers soon develop separation anxiety when left by a parent, without ever having experienced abandonment.

As we grow, we develop strategies for dealing with these natural fears, but we often take on new looming fears and potential dangers that work in our hearts and minds and eventually mold our actions and relationships. Some fears we learn to rationalize, to live with, hoping they never surface to scare the wits out of us. But even our best-laid plans fail to protect us.

So how do we move through life with confidence when all our efforts at creating safe places often crumble without warning?

"I'm sorry, you have cancer. . . ."

"Mom, I'm pregnant. . . ."

"Your son's been shot. . . ."

"You're fired. . . ."

"I'm addicted. . . ."

"Why did I choose to have that abortion?"

And life is never the same again. We don't ask for such blows, nor would we knowingly go back in time and make the same regret-filled decisions that hindsight tells us were wrong.

But still we carry enormous loads of guilt and heartache, running it all through our emotional processors, pulverizing it into a bitter mixture of cynicism, anger, and self-pity. We long for a place to pour out our pain and a place to fill up again with sweet refreshment. So we try to create a sanctuary by sorting out and labeling our feelings. We think if we only get to the root of our pain it will go away. So we spend hours and money to become professional navel gazers only to discover we've created a religion out of our brokenness. And when we step back to look at how we're doing, we see our sanctuary for what it really is—a lean-to hovel full of holes and leaks.

Personally, I need a sanctuary where I can take those feelings and pour them out rather than build a shrine to them. However, there is a danger in seeking God's sanctuary, as well. In the process of coming to him, it's easy to turn the focus on myself. When my prayers revolve around *my* relief, *my* comfort, or *my* peace, then I seek only the gift without desiring to know the Giver of those gifts.

Madeleine L'Engle put it well when she wrote,

> I don't always want freedom. I want security. I want comfort, I want nothing to go wrong, nobody I love to be hurt, to disappoint me. But that is not what Jesus offered. He offered life and life more abundantly, and that means everything, the whole spectrum, laughter and tears, joy and disappointment, but above all, life lived fully and openly and appreciatively. That is how Jesus lived, and how we are to live.[1]

Sanctuary is not a self-help book. It's a "God, help!" book. It won't necessarily free you of your problems, but it will lead you to a place where you can rest from them. In fact, you'll see in the stories of these women that many of them still face the same struggle day in and day out, but they've also found a "rest stop" in God. They've found sanctuary in the One who carries their heartaches and walks with them, day after day.

We all need a safe place, a gentle touch, a resting point to help us persevere when life deals out the unexpected. Otherwise, we're forced to simply live in an emotionally dangerous world where guilt rules, change destroys, loss tortures, and regret kills. There's no need to live in such a world without hope, without courage, or without faith. There's no need, because, as the old hymn says, "There is a place of quiet rest, near to the heart of God."

Rather than tell you what God's sanctuary is like, let me take you on a tour and show you sanctuary through the eyes of women[2] like you and me who have been there and can say, "I'm safe. I'm home free."

Chapter One

SANCTUARY
OF
GRACE

Seventeen ... in love ... at least infatuated, summed up my state of mind. Home alone with my soon-to-be fiancé turned too many minutes of intimacy into foolishness and regret. Enraptured by the moment, I never heard the front door open or my parents walk into the house until it was too late. Caught! Embarrassed, ashamed, wanting to run, grabbing for cover, full of disbelief and panic.

Why? Why did I do it? my mind cried.

That night, after some outward semblance of order had returned, I flopped onto my bed, exhausted by tears and guilt, wondering what punishment awaited me. All I could see was deep hurt in my parents' eyes. All I could feel was an unbearable guilt in my soul. I'd always be sorry, always regret being the one to inflict such pain on us all.

Dad was preparing to go out of town for a weekend speaking engagement. But before he left, he said, "We'll talk about it when I get back. In the meantime, no phone calls or visits." I nodded my understanding. In truth, I was glad to be "grounded." I needed time to think things through.

When Dad returned, he immediately asked to speak to both of us. We sat at the kitchen table like two criminals awaiting judgment. I kept my head low, still feeling embarrassed, hiding like the little girl between the fence and the bush. How I wished I could find a clear way of escape—with no splinters. I wanted to turn back the hands of time and do things over again, only different.

"I've spent most of the weekend praying about this," Dad began. "I know how much you two care about each other." I glanced at him as he continued. "All I can say is, I forgive you."

Shocked. I jerked my head up and met his eyes, trying to discern what he was saying, what he meant. I waited. Even though he said he forgave me, I knew there would still be consequences and punishment to "help me learn the lesson"—at least a morality lecture. Actually, I hoped for a punishment to relieve my own conscience, to pay for what I'd done, to show my parents how much I wanted to make it right.

"What punishment, Dad?" I asked softly.

"No punishment. You're forgiven."

His words knocked the wind out of me. Like a little stone flung from a sling of grace, Dad's simple words slew the giant named Regret already stomping inside me, bullying me, and threatening to defeat me. Even at such a tender age, that grace struck me hard between the eyes, and I knew all at once how much my parents loved me.

If only all my experiences in life fell within the hands of a loving, God-fearing father like my dad. When I go back to that time in my life, I often wonder, *What if. . . ? What if he hadn't forgiven me?* I wonder, *What if. . . ?* when I hear women share similar experiences with much different endings. Some never got caught but lived with other consequences—sexually transmitted disease, unwanted babies, abortions, and motherhood at too early an age. Some felt only wrath, anger, or abandonment by their earthly parents, and they wonder, *What if . . . my father had forgiven me?* But having an earthly father who fails to hand out grace does not preclude our entry into God's grace.

So often we continue, much to our own dismay, to fill that need for grace with more hurt . . . or with men who we hope will meet our need to be accepted. Where can we go with the regret of sin? What penance can we pay to make right the wrong in our hearts? We say we can't get something for nothing. We have to pay. We have to make restitution when we've messed up.

If we begin to ask these kinds of questions, or try to "pay the price," we lock ourselves out of God's sanctuary. God comes with the key, hoping we'll ask him to open the door. But to enter we must leave the shack built with our penance and our good works. We must step out and listen while God turns the key and explains, "There's nothing *you* can do to make it right. Nothing you can say to change how it turns out. There's nowhere you can run and hide to rid yourself of the guilt and regret of bad decisions."

Thankfully, God doesn't leave us out in the cold with that thought. Even though there's nothing *we* can do . . . there's something *he* can do. In fact, he's already done it by letting his Son pay the price for our mistakes. With that key of grace, the dead bolt turns, the latch clicks, and the great doors to God's sanctuary open wide into warmth and light.

As inviting as this place appears, grace creates a problem for us, because we don't live in a world where grace is the norm. From birth, we're taught to be work oriented. We set goals for ourselves to determine if we will succeed or fail. We look for visible results in everything we do, from baking bread to raising children. We spend most of our lives rewarded for being good and punished for being bad, and we define ourselves by how the scales have tipped in our favor or against us.

We expect pay for what we do, and we buy what we need. If we do something for nothing, we at least want to be recognized. The problem is, such a philosophy elbows its way in front of grace. Consequently, we shove grace aside, for four reasons:

We can't earn grace . . .

. . . just like the story of a man named Simon the Sorcerer, who literally tried to buy God's power from Jesus' disciples. To this, Peter the apostle responded, "May your money perish with you, because you thought you could buy the gift of God with money! You have no part or share in this ministry, because your heart is not right before God. Repent of this wickedness and pray to the Lord. Perhaps he will forgive you for having such a thought in your heart. For I see that you are full of bitterness and captive to sin" (Acts 8:20–24).

When regret and guilt hold me captive, I sometimes try to earn the power of God's grace to release me, like Simon did. Only I pay by "being good." Others try to buy God's grace with church attendance or generous giving that they hope someone will notice. How about self-sacrifice? Let's admit it. We women sometimes wear weariness as a badge of honor, a sign of martyrdom, never realizing that God isn't impressed. All he looks for is a broken and contrite heart emptied of self and ready to be filled with his grace.

We don't deserve grace . . .

. . . because we're sinners, and God is not. That's a hard pill to swallow. I remember a cartoon depicting a husband and wife on Judgment Day waiting their turn to stand before God, who has a big open book in front of him. The woman says, "George, please, whatever you do, don't ask for what you have coming to you." God tells us in black and white that we're all sinners—there's no one righteous (Romans 3:10). And there's only one way to buy off the sin—that is to exchange it for death. The wages of sin is death (Romans 6:23). We deserve death for our sin.

But just as we step up to the gallows, Jesus, the perfect Son of God steps into our place. He took upon himself what we deserved. The pure and holy One became dirtied and broken by our sin as he hung on the cross and died for us all. When we accept his death as payment for our sin, we receive forgiveness and eternal life. That's why grace is an undeserved gift.

We don't recognize grace . . .

. . . because today we don't call sin, "sin." We call it a weakness, denial, a blind spot, rebellion, a mistake, or dysfunction. When we do recognize sin, we blow it off like a speck of dust with a comment like "Hey, I'm only human." It may be easy to overlook sin, but if we do, we miss out on grace.

So what have we done with grace? We have replaced it with "healing through counseling" or "developing a strong sense of self-worth." We turn to self-help books. Rather than looking to God, we say to ourselves, "Just deal with it," "Get over it," "Don't worry, time heals." But real healing and recovery isn't about finding answers and building ourselves up. It's about relinquishing control and letting God change us from the inside out. It's about taking our brokenness and sin to God and letting his grace abound in us.

Grace is hard to grasp . . .

. . . like a bar of wet soap. Bible commentator William Barclay illustrates the difficulty of grasping this free gift when he explains that God's grace has to be free for two reasons: God is perfection, and God is love. If God is perfection, then nothing we can do would ever satisfy him. Only perfection is good enough for God, and by our nature this is something we can't offer. And if God is love, then our sin isn't a crime against his law but a crime against love. Sin is not so much breaking God's law as it is breaking God's heart.[1]

Why is it necessary to think about sin and grace and how it all relates to our regret? Is it to send us on a divine guilt trip? To make us feel so badly about having fallen short in God's eyes that we straighten up and fly right? No, that would return us to earning grace by good works. God simply wants us to bring our regrets to the Cross—the Cross he bore to release us from guilt. It is there that he begins to create new life in us.

Here's the good news—Jesus isn't still hanging on the cross. He was raised from death to incorruptible new life. "And God raised us up with Christ and seated us with him in the heavenly realms. . . ." And listen to the reason why: So that "he might show the incomparable riches of his grace, expressed in his kindness to us in Christ Jesus" (Ephesians 2:6–7).

My dad opened the door for me into the treasure room of grace, where he expressed incomparable richness through his kindness and mercy. Looking back over my forty-plus years, I've decided that incident as a young woman of seventeen did more to shape my relationship with Jesus than any other. I have a feeling there may have been more words, more conflict than what I've described here, but it all fades into shadows compared to the shimmering brightness in the sanctuary of grace.

That grace, not the guilt, has followed me to places where my human ability to forgive would have fallen far short. Regret no longer bullies me. Rather, goodness and mercy follow me all the days of my life. All I need do is leave my hovel and ask for the key to enter through those great doors into God's sanctuary of grace.

> *"Surely goodness and mercy will follow me all the*
> *days of my life, and I will dwell in the house*
> *of the Lord forever"*

(Psalm 23:6 KJV).

LIVING DAILY IN GOD'S GRACE

STUDY

Read 1 John 1:8–2:2. Confess (agree with God) that you have sinned.

Read Psalm 103:10–13 as a description of grace. What does God do with your sin once you've given it (confessed it) to him?

Read Ephesians 1:7–10. What aspects of grace, other than forgiveness, are mentioned in this passage?

Many of the New Testament letters begin and end with blessings and prayers of grace to the readers. How can you apply this practice in your daily life as you interact with others?

CONSIDER

Knowing that Jesus already paid the wage of death for you, imagine him speaking to the Father on your behalf. What would he say? How would you respond as you listen to their conversation?

PRAY

Read Isaiah 53:4–6. Personalize this passage with your own name to fully understand the impact of God's grace toward you. Consider how this Scripture addresses grace in every aspect of your life and thank God for each new realization and understanding of his love.

RESPOND

Compile a list of individuals who have extended grace to you in some way.

Take time to let them know, in conversation or in writing,

how their action impacted your life. Continue through your list until you acknowledge each individual, wherever possible.

As you consider these acts of grace, what can you learn in order to deepen your understanding of God's grace?

Chapter Two

SANCTUARY
OF
COMFORT

Sanctuary

My friend Betty hands me a bottle of ketchup, and I instinctively open the lid for her as she talks. Thinking back over her life, she explains, "I felt totally robbed of all my joy. I literally thought I'd never laugh again."

It's hard to believe. Betty is the image of happiness. Her light blue eyes always sparkle. She smiles and laughs at the tiniest pleasures of life. It's nearly impossible to picture this joyful woman unable to laugh. But one look away from her bright eyes and you can't help but notice her gnarled hands. Her stiff gait reveals the pain she endures. Consider the times she calls for help to complete simple tasks, like opening a ketchup bottle. Not many could battle that joy thief called Pain with as much grace as she demonstrates.

As a young woman with a toddler and a newborn, the day arrived that changed Betty's life.

"I woke up one morning with my entire body literally inflamed—every joint red and swollen—and I couldn't get out of bed. Being a nurse, I had a pretty good idea what was going on. So when I finally made it to the doctor several days later, I wasn't surprised when he spoke the words I dreaded to hear . . . rheumatoid arthritis."

Pain clung to Betty like a shadow she couldn't shake.

"I was devastated. I didn't know how I'd take care of my three-year-old daughter and my infant son. I could barely hobble around the house. I pictured myself living from a wheelchair. On top of the pain, the fatigue factor is like an ongoing case of flu."

She fell into a deep sense of apathy, not caring about anything or anyone in particular, simply living in survival mode. Her husband offered undaunting support in every way, but it was an elderly Swedish woman from her church who challenged Betty in a new way. She phoned one day and said, "I want to come and see you."

After she arrived, she immediately began to help with the tasks at hand. As she washed dishes, she said to Betty, "I understand you've been very, very sick. God doesn't want you to live like this. You have children to raise. But you must search the Scriptures." That simple admonition and encouragement turned Betty's life around and set her on a long journey toward the heart of God.

"I fully believe God sent this woman to me," Betty says. "Her words and tenderness and helping hands felt like his love pouring over me and into me." From that moment on, Betty craved God's Word. She couldn't get enough of it. She devoured it in every spare moment and still today calls it her best medicine. She knows now that when this woman said, "God doesn't want you to live like this," she was referring to more than just physical brokenness. She knew God didn't want Betty to live a brokenhearted, joyless life because of the pain she would endure.

People who suffer physically either touch the face of God and enter his sanctuary of comfort, or they throw accusations back in his face and dwell in bitterness. Betty didn't go without her spiritual battles: "At first I had a very shallow view of God. I thought as long as my life was going along beautifully, God was beautiful. But I've learned he disciplines those he loves." (See Hebrews 12:5–11.)

This is where it's easy to lose track of God's sanctuary. When we're dealing with physical suffering, we forget there's more to us than the body, especially when we haven't the strength or desire to even whisper a prayer for help. Unfortunately, when the body that houses the spirit is "broken," the spirit becomes vulnerable to deceptive lies about why we suffer.

For example:

Some people believe we suffer because of sin in our lives. This assumption caused the disciples to ask Jesus about a man blind since birth. "Who sinned, this man or his parents, that he was born blind?" (John 9:1).

Others say, "If my faith were stronger I'd be healed." Whose faith was stronger than Job's? Although he suffered through every aspect of life, still he said, "Though [God] slay me, yet will I hope in him" (Job 13:15). God allowed Job to be tested because of his *strong* faith, not his weak faith.

Still others believe, "It must not be God's will to heal me." In fact, it is completely within God's will for his creation to be whole and redeemed. Sin and suffering were not part of his original plan for us. He does not delight in seeing his children suffer any more than we delight in seeing our own children suffer. "In all their distress he too was distressed" (Isaiah 63:9).

So, why do we suffer? Why aren't we healed when we faithfully follow Christ and desire healing? The sanctuary of comfort uncovers the answer.

Suffering Reveals God's Glory

Return to the moment when Jesus' disciples asked him about the reason for the blind man's condition. "Was this because of the sin of the parents or this man?" they wanted to know.

"Neither," Jesus said. He then revealed a more compassionate way to look at suffering. "You're asking the wrong question," he explained. "You're looking for someone to blame. There is no such cause-effect here. Look instead for what God can do. This happened that the work of God might be displayed in his life" (John 9:3 THE MESSAGE, NIV).

What a relief. We don't have to blame ourselves or anyone else for our suffering. It simply doesn't matter who or what's to blame. When we look to God's comfort and focus on the work he accomplishes through us in the midst of the pain, we experience a new depth of understanding his purpose in us and his comfort toward us. But beyond our own relief, it explains why those who enter the sanctuary of comfort through the door of suffering often consider it an honor to suffer for God's good work and his glory, to be chosen in this way.

Suffering Teaches Us to Trust and Obey

Even Jesus wasn't healed or spared from suffering on the way to the cross. "During the days of Jesus' life on earth, he offered up prayers and petitions with loud cries and tears to the one who could save him from death, and he was heard because of his reverent submission" (Hebrews 5:7).

This reminds us that although God certainly hears our prayers, he doesn't necessarily remove the suffering, not even from his own Son. Here's why: "Although he was a son, he learned obedience from what he suffered" (Hebrews 5:8). Jesus learned obedience! Perfect, sinless Jesus continued a growth process on his journey to understand how to fully love his Father through obedience and submission.

If Jesus learned obedience through his suffering, how much more can we gain as we suffer with him? Like Jesus, we, too, can learn to lay down our lives, to make our bodies living sacrifices, and to endure the suffering. Then we can say at the end of our lives, "It is finished." We needn't cease our prayer for healing, but rather connect it to our prayer to remain faithful and grow in obedience through the hard spots of life.

We Can't Pluck the Rose of Comfort Until It's Grown Up Among the Thorns

When we see Jesus suffer in the hours leading up to the Cross, we, too, suffer, knowing the damage inflicted on his body was a result of our sin. When we empty our sin and suffering at his feet, he fills us with his comfort. He comes alongside us and takes our brokenness upon his own body. We simply cannot separate comfort from the Cross any more than we can separate a rose from its brier and keep the bloom alive. "For just as the sufferings of Christ flow over into our

lives, so also through Christ our comfort overflows" (2 Corinthians 1:5).

Author Tricia McCary Rhodes puts it this way:

> Why did the Lord suffer so? Why didn't He die
> quickly—why the mocking, the torture, the flogging,
> the spitting, and the beating? I know my salvation was
> purchased with His blood shed on Calvary, but what of
> His other wounds? What did they accomplish? . . . In
> order to identify with the suffering of saints throughout
> Christian history, Jesus could not simply march to Cal-
> vary and be executed. *He had to be made like His breth-
> ren in all things.*[1]

God refuses to let one ounce of suffering be inflicted on
our souls without extruding an equal or greater weight of his
goodness and comfort from it as well. Jesus leads the pro-
cession of suffering saints all the way to the Cross. There his
pierced hands hold out our comfort, his thorny punishment
crowns us with peace, and his death gives birth to our forgiveness, mercy, and eternal life.

It's been twenty-five years since the start of Betty's painful journey, but she sees it as a spiritual pilgrimage teaching
her obedience and dependence upon God alone. His Word
continues to comfort her each day: "In every area of my
body where I experience the most pain—my arms, feet,
knees—God's Word touches me." One of her favorite verses
relates to God disciplining those he loves, and it ends with
these words: "Therefore, strengthen your feeble arms and
weak knees. Make level paths for your feet, so that the lame

may not be disabled, but rather healed" (Hebrews 12:12–13).

Betty has learned that God may not bring an outer healing, but his comfort leaves her wondering how else she would intimately know the beauty of his inner sanctuary. Her willingness to turn her pain over to him allows her to touch his face and find compassion and to bathe in his Word and find deep-down soul healing.

Today she exchanges her suffering for Christ's comfort, and her life becomes a "fragrance of the knowledge of him . . . the aroma of Christ . . . the fragrance of life" (2 Corinthians 2:14–16).

Look beyond her gnarled hands and stiff gait and into her smiling eyes. There you'll see her joy rising like the sweet scent of a rose in the midst of the brier.

"We have this treasure in jars of clay to show that this all-surpassing power is from God and not from us. We are hard pressed on every side, but not crushed; perplexed, but not in despair; persecuted, but not abandoned; struck down, but not destroyed. We always carry around in our body the death of Jesus, so that the life of Jesus may also be revealed in our body. For we who are alive are always being given over to death for Jesus' sake, so that his life may be revealed in our mortal body"

(2 Corinthians 4:7–11).

FINDING GOD'S COMFORT THROUGH SCRIPTURE

STUDY

Read Hebrews 4:12–13. List all the areas of life mentioned here that the Word of God touches and enters into. Is there any area of your life excluded from the power of God's Word?

What do you think it means for the Word of God to divide the soul and spirit, joints and marrow?

Now read John 1:1–3, 14. The "Word of God" written about in Hebrews is the same "Word made flesh" spoken of in John 1.

Consider how the Word of God made flesh (Jesus) touches and enters your life. How does Jesus dwelling in you bring you comfort?

CONSIDER

As humans, we all experience pain in one form or another. Is it easier or more difficult for you to recognize God and turn to him in the midst of pain? Why?

PRAY

Read the Twenty-third Psalm. Meditate on the comfort of each phrase and each step you take with the Shepherd. Rewrite this psalm as a personal prayer to God, reflecting on his comfort and thanking him for his provision.

RESPOND

Search the Scriptures daily to find God's sanctuary of comfort as he leads and directs and speaks to you each day.

If daily Bible reading is a new discipline for you, begin by reading John 14–21 over the next several days. These chapters vividly address comfort, pain, and suffering—both our own and Christ's.

Chapter Three

SANCTUARY
OF
ACCEPTANCE

Sanctuary

"Ben says he isn't moving to Illinois with us." Kelly paused, looked away, and bit her lip to keep the tears at bay. "I have to pray all the time, because I feel the bitterness edging its way in. He has no idea how his rejection affects us and hurts his little sister, too. She just sits in Ben's room and plays there for hours. I told him how hard it is on us, and do you know what he said?"

I shook my head no.

"He said, 'Don't lay a guilt trip on me, Mom.'

"I'm sorry, but I think it's time he understood his actions have consequences. If he's big enough to run away from home, he's big enough to face the consequences of his decision." I waited, ready to hear more.

I know how much Kelly and her husband, Jim, love their son, but I can only guess how deep their wounds go. Ben's rebellion started in the typical way. Several work-related moves uprooted the family from homes and friends and communities. This time, fifteen-year-old Ben connected with the wrong crowd—kids who had no parents at home, who took pride in the trouble they caused, and who found fun in breaking the law. Late-night joyrides, drinking, and an attitude of disdain for parents infected Ben's lifestyle and his perception of his family. Many nights he never came home. He slept in parks or at a friend's house without the parents' knowledge.

Between missing person reports and arraignments, Kelly and Jim became well acquainted with police officers and judges' chambers. Regardless of their stance, whether they supported and loved Ben unconditionally, used "tough love" tactics, or ignored his bad behavior, he continued his rebellion. But somehow, in the midst of it all, this high-IQ kid always got himself to school each day and to church youth group on Sunday nights.

When his youth leaders found out he was living on the streets, they intervened and offered to take Ben into their own homes. "We were floored that they were willing to take such a risk," Kelly explained. "I don't know what we would have done without our church family's support. They demonstrated a true love for us and for Ben in their desire to bear this burden with us and for us."

For the past six months Ben has lived with his youth leader, who has taken him under his wing. Meanwhile, Kelly reels under the stress of letting go of her son while maintaining a sense of balance for the rest of the family as they prepare for yet another move. This time it will be without Ben, and Kelly dreads saying good-bye. "When we finally said okay to his staying here, I felt like I was starting all over. All the progress I'd made in accepting the situation crumbled, and I'm back to dealing with a broken heart."

For many parents, such outright rejection from a child

inflicts a mortal wound. But Kelly has found a peace in the midst of this battlefield, even when fresh wounds threaten to tear her family apart.

The pain of rejection runs deep—far beyond the fear of failure in what we *do*. Rejection plunges its dagger into the depths of who we *are*. For Kelly, she hates to consider the possibility that Ben may never accept them or return their love. She asks herself over and over, *What if he never wants to come back?* Like every parent with a rebellious child, she rehashes moments and conversations and life events, searching for where she went wrong. Each remembrance adds to the self-doubts about what she has or has not done for her son.

Rejection taunts us with lies, and bludgeons our minds into believing we're incompetent and unlovable. But if we listen hard, we'll hear the loving voice of our heavenly Father whispering words of acceptance—words that destroy those infectious lies and offer a balm of peace to soothe the piercing wound.

Since the Creation of the world, rejection has stung God's own heart. After he created a home called Paradise, the first man and woman to live there rebelled and rejected God's offer of provision. More than that, they rejected God himself. By their actions, they declared his provision inadequate and opted instead to rule over their own lives on their own terms. When they realized their mistake, they never offered to make things right—they never even said, "We're sorry."

Instead, they masked their error and took cover behind bushes and fig leaves, hoping they stretched far enough to camouflage their sin. But when God confronted them with their rebellious attitudes, they shook their fingers at God and said, in effect, "Don't try to lay a guilt trip on us." They blamed each other, the serpent, and then God.

Indeed, God understands rejection. And so he offers us words of encouragement and hope and acceptance to soothe the sting inflicted by the stroke of rejection.

The Fear of Incompetence

Kelly remembers a time when sleep evaded her for days as she worried over her son's whereabouts and well-being. "Finally, I just had to release him to God and trust him to love my child more than I did. I had to decide that he would use this pain for good in molding Ben to be the person he wants him to be." Sleep came to her immediately after offering up that prayer, but Kelly was surprised when she awoke the next morning and still felt disturbed and troubled.

"I realized there was something else at the heart of my fear. I was afraid that all the years of love and sacrifice I'd given Ben would be lost. I was afraid I simply hadn't done enough for him, and I couldn't live with that realization." That morning, Kelly dragged herself to her weekly Bible study group more depressed and frightened than she'd ever been. But God brought her there for a reason. The Scripture they studied that morning was Hebrews 6:10: "God is not unjust; he will not forget your work and the love you have shown him as you have helped his people and continue to help them."

At that moment, Kelly literally entered the sanctuary of

God's acceptance as she brought her broken and fearful heart to her loving Father. She cried over his tender and complete acceptance of all she was and all she wasn't. In that verse, God confirmed that he not only saw her work of being a mother to Ben as competent and sufficient, but he also counted it as an act of love toward Ben and toward God himself. Her faithful mothering would continue to equip Ben, even if he continued to reject her.

"What also amazed me was the footnote in my Bible that made me feel like God had placed it there just for me." It said, "It's easy to get discouraged thinking God has forgotten us. But God is never unjust. He never forgets or overlooks our hard work for him. Presently you may not be receiving rewards and acclaim, but God knows your efforts of love and ministry. Let God's love for you and his intimate knowledge of your service for him bolster you as you face disappointment and rejection here on earth."[1]

Those words continue to comfort Kelly and remind her that God has already accepted her works and loves who she is regardless of what she has or has not done.

The Fear of Being Unlovable

When we've given our all to someone and that individual rejects our overtures of love, it's hard not to think we may simply be unworthy of love. But when we look at God in light of the rejection he has endured, we see that rejection doesn't change who the person is. Whether humanity acknowledges him or not, he is still the only one to be praised and worshiped.

Even if all creation rejected God, he remains holy and just and pure and majestic and sovereign and worthy of our love. The world's denial of God's love doesn't make him into an unlovable ogre. This truth is illuminated to a brilliance at the Cross. There the world fully rejected Jesus. Tortured until he was unrecognizable in his disfigurement, he never ceased to be the Son of God (Isaiah 52:14; 53:3). It doesn't change the fact that he is still Wonderful Counselor, Mighty God, Everlasting Father, Prince of Peace (Isaiah 9:6). Our rejection didn't turn him into a sacrificial failure.

Likewise, when someone we love rejects us, it doesn't change the beauty of who God created us to be. It doesn't change the fact that we are God's children. We make false assumptions when we equate someone's acceptance or rejection of us as a definition of our worth. For Kelly, rejection by a child does not change the fact that she is still that child's mother. It does not change the fact that she loves her son. And understanding that truth shines the light of God's accepting love back into her heart.

The move to Illinois was tense. "When we said our goodbyes to Ben the night before we left, it felt like I had torn off a part of me and left it behind—like one of those strange nightmares when something gruesome happens but everyone goes on with life as though it didn't matter."

But despite the painful experience of Ben's rebellion, Kelly clings closer to God. It's spurred her on to consider her own areas of rebellion toward God. "Since this all began, I've felt led by God to physically kneel in my prayer time as a symbol of submission to him. It's hard for me to want to do that. But that simple gesture makes me feel like I'm soothing his rejected heart. I know that pain, and if I can ease

God's pain by kneeling before him, then I'll be forever on my knees."

And as she offers herself in the sanctuary of acceptance, God soothes the sting of rejection and smoothes the jagged edge of bitterness that threatens to cut into her soul.

"But God has surely listened and heard my voice in prayer. Praise be to God, who has not rejected my prayer or withheld his love from me!"

(Psalm 66:19–20).

DEALING WITH A REBELLIOUS HEART

STUDY

Read Isaiah 30:15–16. How does verse 16 describe God's sanctuary? How does it describe rebellion against God? Have you ever run from God? What draws you away from him?

Now read verses 18–21. In the midst of the rebellion, what is God's attitude and action?

In quietness ask God to reveal areas of rebellion in your own life. Could this be the "bread of adversity and the water of affliction" mentioned in verse 20?

How can verse 15 help you submit to God's love and enter into his sanctuary? If you've been rejected by someone with a rebellious heart, how does this verse help you respond to that person?

CONSIDER

Most rebellion is a reaction of fear—fear of losing control, fear of losing our rights, fear of being asked to do something we may hate to do. In the areas of life where you feel rebellious, consider what the underlying fear may be. Ask God to help you cast out those fears and trust him wholeheartedly with your life.

PRAY

In your prayer time today, kneel before God in an attitude of submission and obedience. Praise him for his graciousness, his compassion, his justice, and his blessing in your life. Remain silent as you wait for him and listen for his voice behind you saying, "This is the way; walk in it" (Isaiah 30:21).

RESPOND

In your journal, write down any new insights gained from your study and prayer time.

How has God opened your eyes and ears to the lessons he has for you?

Take time to share these thoughts with your spouse, a trusted friend, or your pastor.

Chapter Four

SANCTUARY
OF
TRUTH

Sanctuary

"I struggle to remember the month, let alone the day, it happened. My brain has shut it out for so long that it's hard to pull out the memory in much detail. I wish I could say, 'My child would have been so many years old this month,' but to be honest, I barely remember the year when I had the abortion." Although Sara can't remember the date, she can't forget the look of horror on the doctor's face who performed the abortion. "It was as if he wanted to say, 'Why are you doing this?'"

Just a few weeks earlier, when she told her boyfriend she was pregnant, she hoped and prayed he loved her enough to do the right thing. But his cold response squelched any joy beginning to rise in her. "You're in college, and no one is going to want to marry you. You're going to ruin your life if you keep that baby." Those fears and lies, along with his assurances that he would arrange everything and take care of her, led to the decision she's regretted every day of her life since.

"I know I was ultimately responsible for the decision, but

how I wish there had been just one person who said, 'Do you realize you have other choices? Do you realize that God loves you?' But nobody did. I knew better, but that part of me seemed to be stuffed deep down, consumed by fear. I felt like an empty shell as I allowed other people to pull me through that nightmare."

The day of the abortion, not only did Sara's baby die, but she buried a part of herself in a grave of denial and fear of what others would think. "I lived in fear for a long time because I felt very alone. My boyfriend deserted me the same afternoon of the abortion. I never saw him or heard from him for over a year. I knew there wasn't anybody I felt safe with. And I felt ashamed."

At first she cried and mourned. But eventually the tears gave way to disbelief, and disbelief to a numbness toward life: "as if a part of me just died." So she closed the coffin and nailed it shut, locking in the hurt and shame and emptiness. She separated that inner part of herself from her outer person.

Only once during the past ten years did Sara look inside and share the truth about her abortion—that was with her future husband, who has loved and supported her through it all. His love has helped her uncover her pain as God shines the light of truth on who she really is.

Why does God want us to unbury the past pains we've tried so hard to forget? Haven't we suffered enough? The fact is, we suffer much more when we hide our sins. These hidden secrets insidiously work behind closed doors in the dark and musty memories we try to ignore. We can't begin to know the damage that denial inflicts on our spiritual, mental, and physical health.

Sara explained, "I find it easy to understand in my head that God has forgiven me, but I'm not sure it has fully penetrated my heart. Knowing that a life was in my hands and I allowed it to be destroyed—I still can't believe I was capable of something like that. I can't forgive myself." And that's how denial begins to destroy us. It tears us up inside so that we can't fully enter the reality of God's truth and love.

Like Sara, King David intellectually recognized God's forgiveness for his sin. But he also understood that real healing was more than a head knowledge of God's mercy: "Blessed is the man whose sin the Lord does not count against him *and* in whose spirit is no deceit" (Psalm 32:2, emphasis added).

Deceit and denial speak through a voice of silence, and that silence wreaks havoc on the body. David said, "When I kept silent, my bones wasted away through my groaning all day long . . . my strength was sapped as in the heat of summer" (Psalm 32:3–4). But when he brought the sin out in the open, God imparted great blessings to him: "I will instruct you and teach you in the way you should go; I will counsel you and watch over you" (Psalm 32:8).

God doesn't ask us to exhume our hurts so he can inflict more pain. He longs to resurrect our deadened hearts with new life. He's waiting to lead us into a wholeness that reconnects and rebuilds our souls. How do we enter the sanctuary of truth where disjointed parts of our being are rejoined into a whole, healthy person? How do we begin to receive his blessing of truth?

Stop Self-Protecting

Sara often wonders how others would react if they knew her secret. "It's hard to consider telling someone about my abortion because there's a fear of how they'll look at me. And even if they say they still love me, I worry that they may wonder what kind of a person I really am." That's the kind of fear we use to protect ourselves and our perceived good reputation. So we struggle to preserve the part of us that people accept by denying the truth of what they may reject.

Such logic, even on a subconscious level, makes fear the undertaker of our souls, ready to bury the joy of living. And when we allow fear to exert such control, we deny God's lordship over us, even over our hurts. In essence we're saying, "I can't trust you, God, because if you expose this with the light of your truth, you're going to hurt me deeper."

Those self-protecting lies of denial keep the coffin closed to God's truth. But Jesus longs to open the lid and escort us into the sanctuary of truth. He said, "I am the way . . ." (John 14:6). He paves a path for our sin to travel toward holiness. When we're willing to stop protecting ourselves, then we're free to run down that path to the only safe place and claim as David did, "*You* are my hiding place; *you* will protect me from trouble and surround me with songs of deliverance" (Psalm 32:7, emphasis added).

Remove the Masks

It's easy to look good and pure and holy on the outside, but to experience God's holiness on the inside requires another step. David went through this process after admitting his sin. That's when he recognized God's desire that truth reign "in the inner parts" of who he was (Psalm 51:6).

God doesn't want our impure or insincere "burnt offerings" or any other religious actions or words that supposedly make us look good on the outside (Psalm 51:16). "If we claim to have fellowship with [God] yet walk in the darkness, we lie and do not live by the truth" (1 John 1:6). By claiming fellowship with God while denying the sin inside and hiding it from others, we mask our pain with religious attitudes. God desires someone honest enough to bring a broken heart into his light. Does God delight in the sacrifice of a broken heart because he is a sadistic God? No, of course not. He delights in it because it allows him to fully express his love to us as his children.

When we remove the mask and enter the sanctuary of truth, two things happen: "we have fellowship with one another, and the blood of Jesus . . . purifies us from all sin" (1 John 1:7). The light of God's truth, which we so often fear may destroy our relationships with others, actually unites us with them in fellowship because it puts us back into the reality that "all have sinned" (Romans 3:23) and "there is no one righteous" (Romans 3:10). The only way to inner holiness is through the Cross of Christ. Jesus said, "I am the truth. . . ." If we fail to remove our mask of self-righteousness, then we'll never look in horror at our sin. And if there is no horror to our separation from God because of that sin, then we will fail to comprehend the passionate love God has toward his creation.

That's a truth Sara is just beginning to understand. She remembers seeing a painting that has helped her visualize that tender love. "It was a picture of a little girl sitting at Jesus' feet with her head resting in his lap. And Jesus is stroking her hair. His eyes reflect an undeniable expression of love. I picture myself as that little girl, that part of me that I buried, and I feel like maybe there is hope."

Move Into New Life

God's truth always leads to hope and to new life. Following Jesus' words "I am the way, I am the truth . . . ," he concluded by saying, "I am the life." In Christ we are born into a new life and we become a new creation (2 Corinthians 5:17–19). When we follow the way God leads us, he takes us into the sanctuary of truth, where we fling open the closed coffins of secret heartaches.

When we uncover our brokenness and willingly hand it over to Christ, we become a living sacrifice, fully alive and whole with no part of our hearts buried in denial or fear. In such a condition, the apostle Paul explained, God renews our minds (Romans 12:1–2). The word *renew* means to renovate. We become God's remodeling project. He takes the buried and broken spirit and body and mends the parts back into one piece, renovating our attitudes, our hearts, and even restoring our physical health. Then we're able to move to the next step. David's repentance and acceptance of God's truth led to his desire to teach others from his own mistakes so that "sinners will turn back to you" (Psalm 51:7).

Sara longs for a new life that can make a difference for other young women in similar situations. But first, she's working on opening the lid of denial that has trapped her for so long. Although she'll never forget her heartache, she knows she'll always experience God's mercy through it. In the past year she's opened her heart to share the truth with two trusted friends.

"It hasn't healed me all at once, but there is something liberating going on. God's given me people willing to hold my hand through it. I'm not sure where it will lead, but I know I have a great desire to be that one person who says to someone, 'Do you realize you have another choice? Do you know how much God loves you?' I'm willing to take that stand and to be those loving arms I know God wants me to be."

With each step away from denial, Sara prays she'll enter deeper into the sanctuary of God's truth. There she can safely fling open the closed doors of dark and musty memories and let the light of his truth flood over her soul.

"Lord, who may dwell in your sanctuary? Who may live on your holy hill? He whose walk is blameless and who does what is righteous, who speaks the truth from his heart. . . . He who does these things will never be shaken"

(Psalm 15:1–2, 5).

Understanding the Paradox of Truth

Study

Read 2 Corinthians 12:7–10. What happens to your weakness or the torment when you turn it over to Christ?

What do you consider a "thorn in the flesh"?

According to these verses, what attitude should you take toward your "thorn in the flesh"?

What truth is revealed about Christ in the passage? What truth is revealed about your own life?

Consider

Think about how Christ might shine through your weakness or your heartache either now or in the future. If you are unable to imagine this, read Romans 8:28, and simply trust his promise to work a good outcome from any and every situation.

Pray

Slowly read Psalm 32 several times. Let the words penetrate your heart. David ends his prayer by saying, "Rejoice . . . be glad . . . sing." In your journal, list reasons why you can rejoice in God's sanctuary of truth as described in this psalm. Take time today to sing to him.

Respond

If you have never shared your secret heartache with anyone, make plans to do so today.

If you have shared the truth with someone, let them know about any new insights you've discovered in God's sanctuary.

Chapter Five

SANCTUARY
OF
ADOPTION

Sanctuary

At age eleven, when most little girls wonder if pink or peach lipstick looks best, Maggie wondered, *Why did Daddy have to die?* And while most of her friends tried to balance on their first pair of heels, Maggie teetered on the edge of despair when she found out her father had committed suicide.

"I had lots of questions, lots of hurt, lots of anger, and didn't know what to do with most of it," she says. "My mom helped me as best she could, but both she and my brother were angry, too. We had so much conflict inside us and between us. My brother and I constantly fought, and I took my anger out on my mother, blaming her for Daddy's death."

Mostly, though, Maggie hid in her bedroom. Her tiny eight-by-nine-foot corner room became the one place of solace and safety—a place to cry, or punch a pillow, or dream of better days to come. Sheer white curtains framed the windows on two walls. When the sun shone through, it bathed the room in softness and light. It literally became a bright spot in her otherwise dark world, a place to settle in and be at home.

She remembers her father as a distant, uncommunicative man, probably an alcoholic, "but he had a sense of humor—maybe his only outlet for dealing with his problems." Intellectually, she accepts his human brokenness and his inability to cope with life, whatever the reasons. But emotionally, she can't ignore the pain.

It's a loneliness that's hard to put away and forget. That feeling of abandonment also makes it difficult to embrace the reality of God as a loving Father, because deep down there's a fear that God will leave, too, that disappointment and hurt are just around the corners of life.

Most of us equate God's character with our perception of our earthly fathers. That's why we need to allow God to disconnect us from the pain of abandonment. We may feel like orphans as a result of divorce, death, neglect, abuse, or any other reason. But we can reconnect our hearts with the perfect Father-heart of God as we enter the sanctuary of adoption.

Adoption occurs only when a parent-child relationship has been severed. In a spiritual sense, that relationship with God fell to pieces when sin separated us from him in the Garden. What we sometimes forget is that when God created Adam and Eve as his children, it wasn't God who broke off the relationship, but the children. They chose to leave him, to distance themselves from him in their rebellion. But in doing so, they missed out on the beauty and depth of that *Abba*-Father relationship. (*Abba* is the Aramaic word for "Daddy.") They walked out of the safety found in God's fatherhood and entered the darkness as orphans.

Even though we reject him, God leaves the door to his sanctuary open for any child who chooses to come home. His adoption goes beyond a mere "Okay, I'll take you back and endure you," in the way we sometimes tolerate difficult family members out of obligation. He wants to reknit and restore the original relationship. Even when we've hurt him, he wants to lavish us with love because we're his children (1 John 3:1).

The story of the prodigal son paints a beautiful picture of reentering a relationship with God through the sanctuary of adoption (Luke 15:11–32). According to the traditions of that time, if a child asked for his inheritance, he, in fact, proclaimed his father dead, disowning the relationship. Symbolically, he killed his father and chose to make himself an orphan. That's why it's so amazing that when the son returns, the father willingly runs to him and lavishes him with love and attention.

We, too, remain fatherless orphans when we choose to disown God's promise and turn our backs on his desire to be our Father. If we choose not to embrace the Father or allow him to come into our emptiness, we miss out on his blessings. Consider what God's adoption offers:

We Can Cut the Natural Connection to a Hurtful Past

Under early Roman law, the adopted child could no longer inherit from his natural father, nor was he liable for any debts. That's astounding news for us as we consider being adopted by God. It means we don't have to inherit a legacy of dysfunction filled with pain, abuse, neglect, or abandonment. We don't have to pay for the hurt inflicted by the world.

The word *adoption* comes from two Greek words. The first word means to settle and sink down into an active position. The second word means immediate kinship. When we allow ourselves to sink down and settle into our relationship with God as our Father, he severs our natural connection to our brokenness by placing us into an active, immediate kinship.

So often we think that God's timing means waiting long and hard for him to decide what he's going to do. But in the case of adoption, he says, "You don't have to wait on me because I can't wait for you to be my child. I choose you right now!" Like a child who jumps into her father's arms the second he arrives home, that reunion of parent and child is immediate.

With an offer like that, why do we hesitate to ask God to reconnect those severed relationships and broken cords directly into his heart? Why do we say it's too hard to fully and immediately become his child in every sense of the word—to be loved, disciplined in love, and encouraged in our growth?

We Have a Father Who Cannot Forsake Us

Ten years after her father's death, while away at college, Maggie met Jesus through an on-campus ministry. As she grew in Christ, she began to come to terms with her father's suicide. By the time she turned twenty-eight, she was ready to begin her own family with her new husband. Life finally felt right. Then, unexpectedly, news came that her mom had died of heart failure at age sixty-four.

Maggie felt like a grown-up orphan and in many ways still feels that sense of abandonment today. "My birthday is the hardest. That's when I feel the most alone." Looking down at her two-month-old son cradled in her arms, she adds, "Who remembers the details of the day you were born besides your mom and dad? Even with my husband and children around me, I somehow feel alone on my birthday."

Although we may feel abandoned, God cannot forsake us. To do so would deny his faithful character. It would deny his promise to never leave us or forsake us (Joshua 1:5). If he did forsake us, he would be a liar, and God cannot lie (Hebrews 6:18).

Maybe the best picture of this truth is when Christ cried out, "My God, my God, why have you forsaken me?" (Mark 15:34). Maggie remembers an Easter weekend when those words comforted her as she realized Jesus completely understood her feelings of being forsaken by a parent.

Some say God turned his back on Jesus at that moment when our sin came to rest upon his Son. But how can that be when his Word says nothing can separate us from his love? (Romans 8:38–39). Perhaps Jesus' cry simply expressed his *feeling* of being forsaken as he lived through despair and pain, hanging on a cross, wounded for our sakes. Our burden of sin temporarily blinded Jesus from seeing God's presence, but it never severed God from his only Son.

God did not abandon Jesus and neither will he abandon us. Christ's resurrection is proof of that. God would have left him in the grave if the sin he bore had caused permanent separation. And he does not forsake us when we sin or even when the sin of others damages us in some way, as it did Christ. Rather, he restores and corrects and teaches us through it all. He loved us, even while sin muddied our souls (Romans 5:8).

"Can a mother forget the baby at her breast and have no compassion on the child she has borne? Though she may forget, I will not forget you! See, I have engraved you on the palms of my hands; your walls are ever before me" (Isaiah 49:15).

If we stop and ask, "Lord, let me see my name engraved on your palms," he opens his hands and shows us his nail-scarred palms, the sign and seal of his willingness to adopt us as his own children.

We Have a Rich Inheritance

Maggie fights back tears today when she considers how much she lost as a result of not having a father during her adolescent years. "I don't know what it's like to have a daddy to take me to a ball game or camping. I don't know what it's like to have a daddy nearby who would help me with my algebra. He didn't leave me an inheritance of faith. I can't even imagine it."

She could list a dozen other life experiences she wishes she could have shared with him. Instead, she looks at the few photos of her dad, the only physical remembrance she has of him, and wonders why he chose to leave his family.

As God's adopted children, we don't have to wonder

about his faithfulness to us. Daily he provides gifts and a rich inheritance expressed to us through the promises of Scripture.

First, *he gives us a new start at life and a living hope*: "Praise be to the God and Father of our Lord Jesus Christ! In his great mercy he has given us *new birth* into a living hope through the resurrection of Jesus Christ from the dead, and into an inheritance that can never perish, spoil or fade— kept in heaven for you" (1 Peter 1:3–5, emphasis added).

Next, *he builds us up in grace to make us a family with all his other adopted children*: "Now I commit you to God and to the word of his grace, which can build you up and give you an inheritance among all those who are sanctified" (Acts 20:32). What a priceless gift for the orphan to be placed in a family that will build her up rather than tear her down!

Then, *he gives us a deposit to guarantee his future inheritance in the life to come*: "Having believed, you were marked in him with a seal, the promised Holy Spirit, who is a deposit guaranteeing our inheritance until the redemption of those who are God's possession—to the praise of his glory" (Ephesians 1:13–14).

Finally, it's not only the new start, the grace, and the future hope, but *God himself is our inheritance*, and we are his as well. The words of the father in the story of the prodigal son express this idea: "My child," the father said, "you are always with me, and everything I have is yours." He said this not to the runaway son but to his other son who was jealous and bitter about the party his father was throwing for his wayward brother.

How sad that this son missed the true beauty of his inheritance. Jealousy blinded him to the fact that his richness lay not in possessions, but in being in relationship with his Father. To always be with the Father is life itself. He is our inheritance. In him we have the right to come home to his sanctuary, the right to share in his riches and his suffering, the right to use his power over evil in our lives, and the right to live forever with him.

Fatherhood may be a hard thing to grasp, but that doesn't negate the relationship or God's position as our heavenly Father through Jesus' sacrifice. We must decide. Do we miss out on the richness of this relationship? Or do we come and embrace him as our Father? What joy that would bring to his heart. And what joy we would finally know if we laid down our pain long enough to enter his sanctuary.

"It's not easy for me to enter that sanctuary," Maggie admits. "But that's the hope I cling to." God is the good Father, able to keep promises, unable to forsake us. And he reassures his frightened daughter that even though it's tough now in this life, someday it will be all right. With that reassuring hope we can take the first steps into the one place of solace and safety, a sanctuary full of softness and light. Rest there and sink into the heart of the Father's tender love.

"I will not leave you as orphans; I will come to you"

(John 14:18).

Enjoying the Fatherhood of God

Study

Imagine the ideal father. How does he act? What does he do for his children and how does he speak to them?

Now read James 1:17–18. How does this describe God's fatherhood? How does he act? What does he do for and say to his children?

How is this description of God the Father similar to your ideal father image? How is it different?

Whether you have a good relationship with your earthly father or not, how is God different from your earthly father? Thank God for being the Father you always dreamed of.

Consider

What you just imagined as the perfect father is only the tip of the iceberg compared to God's unfathomable love for you. Now consider that Ephesians 3:20 says God is able to do immeasurably *more* than all we can ever ask or imagine according to his power at work in us.

Pray

Meditate on each point of the inheritance God gives his children. Pray over the Scriptures given. If you do not yet feel comfortable with the fatherhood of God, take some time to communicate your feelings to him. Write down what scares you about that relationship. Ask him to redirect your heart to the truth of what it means for him to be your Father. Use a journal to record your thanks to him for walking with you through this process.

RESPOND

Share with another woman your struggles or joys of knowing God as Father.

Ask her how she sees God.

Pray for God's power to be at work in both of you as you learn to enjoy the heavenly Father.

Chapter Six

SANCTUARY
OF
COMPASSION

Sanctuary

She knew she should cry at her beloved husband's funeral. But Deb blotted away the tears before they ever had a chance to fall. She'd already said her good-byes to Eddie and wept enough during his final days to fill fountains. To be honest, today she felt proud to have made it through this valley of death and to finally count herself among the living again.

Her steel gray eyes reflected her self-confidence. With a knowing smile she reassured her two children that all would be well. Certainly God wouldn't begrudge her those feelings of hope and anticipation even as they lay her husband to rest. But for some reason she couldn't get Eddie's words out of her head: *"I realize I've always relied on my own ability to trust God more than I've relied on God himself."* Those words rang out like a starting gun for a race. And she felt ready to sprint into a new life and away from this grief.

Deb had every reason to grieve. Twelve years into their marriage, Eddie was diagnosed with lung cancer. "At first I was overwhelmed by his helplessness and the pain he was experiencing. I had never seen him in a situation where he needed anything from me or anyone else." But after the surgeon removed the cancer, Eddie quickly learned there was a spiritual problem with his own strong-willed self-reliance. That's when he told Deb those words that echoed through her mind during his funeral. They would prove to be profound and prophetic in her own journey toward God.

Throughout the ordeal, she remained strong for her family's sake. "I know God provided the strength I needed to maintain a normal life for everyone. But at the same time, I kept him at a safe distance. I relied on myself emotionally and lived in denial in a lot of ways. I actually taught a Bible study class the day before Eddie died, pretending I was handling everything just fine. These were the emotional boundaries I set for myself. And God, in his great compassion, allowed me that space."

After Eddie's initial surgery, life returned to normal for almost a year. But a lingering bout with flu led him back to the doctors. They eventually discovered the cancer had invaded his liver and lymph nodes. From that day, Deb lived with Eddie's cancer and helped him battle it until his death just eleven months later at the age of forty-one.

At first the relief and freedom from the burden of caring for a terminally ill husband energized her. "At that point I wasn't grieving. I wanted to help my children through it, even though I was ready to get on with my life." But at the same time, Deb's ability to run from the pain kept God and his compassion always in pursuit of her heart.

Webster's defines compassion as "consciousness of others' distress together with a desire to alleviate it." However,

God's compassion goes a step further. He doesn't just *desire* to ease the distress. In Hebrew, *compassion* involves an actual touching and handling and entering into a physical realm to provide through the distress. That's the compassion described in Scripture when God helped the Israelites survive in the wilderness. He instructed them and physically provided food, water, shelter, even the ever new sandals on their feet. He gave them a home, fulfilled his promises, and always forgave them whenever they turned to him (Nehemiah 9:19–27).

When Deb finally stopped and allowed herself to grieve, she began to understand that her needs, her weaknesses, and even her self-reliant strength could never outdistance God's untiring compassion (Lamentations 3:22). She knew he was conscious of her distress and would meet her deepest needs. He provided for her in surprising ways as his compassion ran stride for stride with her grief.

God's Compassion Leads Us

Once during Eddie's bout with the flu and before his final diagnosis of terminal cancer, Deb awoke in the middle of the night from a vivid dream: "I believed God was speaking to me. Somehow, I knew the cancer had spread, was affecting the liver, and Eddie would die from it. I knew he had only a few months. I cried myself back to sleep that night, but didn't tell anyone about the dream."

The flu symptoms led to gallbladder surgery and the discovery of the spreading cancer. "When the surgeon came out and told me, 'We have some bad news . . .' I thought I was going to pass out, even though I knew in my heart what I'd hear. I've always been grateful that God prepared me for it. He knew just what I would need to handle those words, and his compassion led me to that truth ahead of time as he guided me through that moment."

God's Compassion Allows Us to Be Human

As much as Deb struggled to maintain her composure and feared losing control, she recalls one time when she told God she couldn't go any further. "I just couldn't deal with Eddie, or his cancer, or the pressures any longer. It was making me crazy. I was a jogger, and I went out for a run early one morning and found myself screaming and crying as I jogged through the countryside."

During that time, something changed inside her. There in the midst of the cornfields, she stopped running ahead of God. She relinquished her fear and allowed God's compassion to catch up to her grief. "I told God I was willing to do whatever he required, regardless of the outcome. When I came home, I was free. I never felt burdened like that again."

Deb realizes now how much God honored her human feelings during those days. His compassion let her choose her emotional pace, even though that pace kept her at a distance from him. It's easy to think that God wants us to be perfect little reflections of who he is. Yet in his compassion "he knows how we are formed, he remembers that we are dust" (Psalm 102:14). And as he remembers, he showers us with compassion and grace in our humanness.

God's Compassion Speaks to Us in Our Weakness

Deb sat in the hospital for days on end with Eddie. In those hours she searched her Bible for God's voice in the midst of insurance battles and medical heartbreak. He spoke to her as she repeatedly turned to his Word for strength. "When I called, you answered me; you made me bold and stouthearted. . . . Though I walk in the midst of trouble, you preserve my life. . . . The Lord will fulfill his purpose for me; your love, O Lord, endures forever—do not abandon the works of your hands" (Psalm 138:3, 7–8).

Those words helped her in practical ways through Eddie's last days. "There are constant obstacles and demands in the treatment of cancer—keeping someone comfortable and communicating what you need and want in the medical environment. God literally made me 'bold and stouthearted' to deal with all that. He provided the stamina I needed for those months. And he gave me hope that he would not abandon me when it was all over. I was certain he would provide for me, and I fully expected him to do that. I knew he had a plan for me, and he would walk me through it."

God's Compassion Lets Us Experience Pain in Order to Become Whole

What Deb didn't realize is that part of God's plan to walk her through it was not always a "comforting compassion." God's compassion doesn't placate us with shallow comfort. Nor does he numb us to take away the pain and fear. His promise that we should have life and have it more abundantly (John 10:10) means providing a path toward our highest benefit in the long run. Just as a parent must push a child toward independence at times, and just as a mother bird pushes a baby bird out of its nest at the right time, so God allowed Deb to go through the suffering of grief to become emotionally healthy at the perfect time.

The last days of Eddie's life were filled with extraordinary love and encouragement and a deep sense of loss all rolled into one. Family members and dozens of friends gathered around him to say good-bye. In private, Eddie told Deb, "I wanted to grow old with you and be there to help with the kids. I know God gave you to me to see me through this. I can't imagine going through it with anyone else." He encouraged Deb in her ability to carry on after he was gone. It was a time when spoken words erased any lingering regrets in life. But the emotional pain of such a loss drained her, even as she continued to put on a show of strength.

Having existed in that environment of death and dying for eleven months, Deb admits she wasn't ready to fully grieve. She longed to return to the land of the living first. "I made a lot of changes. I took the kids on a couple of trips, moved from the country into town, enrolled in college to finish my education, remodeled the house, and generally kept moving so grief couldn't catch up to me."

The emotional danger in losing a loved one exists not in the grieving, but rather in ignoring the need to embrace it. Eighteen months after her husband's death, grief began expressing itself in subtle but unhealthy ways. At first Deb couldn't figure out what was happening to her. She felt angry and stressed most of the time. She had intense dreams of

Eddie betraying her or dying again and again, and she felt enraged. Slowly that anger surfaced into reality with cynical and caustic attitudes and words. "When I realized I was going to have to grieve, I was angry about that, too. I believed I had been through enough. I was not willing to be depressed and sad again."

Deb could no longer ignore the grief bottled up inside her. For the next fifteen months she cried over her loss. She dropped all her classes except one. "When I wasn't in class, I would sit or slump and gaze into space or sleep on the couch. When the children were home, I did what had to be done." Finally she was able to admit she couldn't do it all. She wasn't equipped for single parenting and had to learn to let others help fill in the gaps.

Recently, ten years after Eddie's death, she realized she still had a final race to run with her grief. "I harbored a forgotten anger toward God for letting my children's father die. They were so small and needed their dad. They needed their world to be secure. It didn't seem fair that they had to hurt and experience that sadness." But having faced those feelings and turned them toward God's sanctuary of compassion, Deb is able to say, "I forgive you, God, for not doing things my way." She finally grieved over her children's loss and believes she's crossed the finish line in a long, hard run.

"I am so grateful to God, not for comforting me in grief so much as for teaching me how to grieve. Learning to grieve and experience pain has blessed me greatly and freed me tremendously. I know the depth of God's compassion when I read the words 'Blessed are those who mourn . . .'" (Matthew 5:4).

Today, Deb looks back and says, "Before this experience I was stoic, and too much of me was buried. I am a more compassionate person because of this grief and because of the new way God has revealed himself to me." It's so much easier to rely on God to set the pace in the grieving process and to let him lead the race to wholeness and healing. What Eddie learned in a short time, Deb finally claims as truth in her own life—"I can no longer rely on my own ability to trust God, but rather God himself is all I can rely upon."

Deb is quick to see grief in others and to react when she senses someone struggling with loss. She picks up her pace to come alongside them, fueled by her knowledge that God's compassion never stops pursuing the grieving heart.

"Praise the Lord, O my soul, and forget not all his benefits . . . who redeems your life from the pit and crowns you with love and compassion, who satisfies your desires with good things so that your youth is renewed like the eagle's"

(Psalm 103:2, 4–5).

TAKING TIME TO GRIEVE

STUDY

Read John 11:17–36. In what ways does Jesus reveal God's compassion to Mary and Martha?

How does Christ's compassion encompass the Hebrew definition of compassion?

Mary and Martha each responded differently to life. How did Martha handle her grief compared to Mary?

Consider how Christ's compassion allowed them each to grieve in their own way.

CONSIDER

We experience many kinds of loss in life: death of a loved one, divorce (either personally or in the life of someone close to us), loss of a child through divorce or separation, loss of a friend through a move or change of work, loss of opportunities because of disease or handicap. Think about whether you have taken time to grieve over your losses.

PRAY

Read Psalm 103:2–5 again. Paraphrase it into a personal prayer. Which words or phrases mean the most to you? Tell God how they make you feel and why.

RESPOND

Allow God to continue speaking to you in the quietness of the moment or through his Word.

Ask him how he wants you to deal with your losses.

Spend a day alone on retreat with God to remember the individual you lost and to rest in God's compassion.

Chapter Seven

SANCTUARY
OF
PEACE

Sanctuary

Anne puts the finishing touches on her turkey sandwich and sits down by herself for a quick lunch. But her ordinary activity is thwarted once again by extraordinary feelings of loneliness. Unable to ignore the lump in her throat and the familiar panic rising inside, her emotions splash over into her routine day. She covers her face with her hands and sobs.

Every day Anne lives with feelings of isolation. Like a child who's lost her way home, sometimes she actively searches for her safe place within the world, a place where others will embrace her and bring an end to this loneliness. At other times, in a solitary moment, an unexpected rush of tears and heartache send her into a panic. All she can do is stop and cry as she wonders when it will all end.

For the last five-and-a-half years Anne has been stranded by loneliness. Her marriage crumbled years earlier, but she's grown accustomed to being single and has even learned to enjoy the freedom it brings. Her daughter, now grown and with a family of her own, lives out of state.

Anne's one connection to life beyond her daughter was her church home group. They were the people who understood her, prayed with her, and encouraged her. So she moved into the bustling city to be closer to her church and also to build her home-business client base. But then unforeseen problems, the resignation of the pastor, and human nature in the midst of turmoil led to the closing of the church.

With time, Anne has worked through the hurt and anger of feeling abandoned again by close friends. Now all that remains is a raw feeling of loneliness that touches every aspect of her life—physical, emotional, and spiritual.

She actively searches for another church family but has found no place to settle in and call home. Week after week she visits and revisits churches in the area, hoping to find the place where God wants her to be. Meanwhile, the expensive metropolitan area where she lives has forced more and more of her old friends to move out of state. Anne helplessly watches them go.

It's been difficult to share her feelings with others. Many Christians quote Scripture to her. "Let us not give up meeting together, as some are in the habit of doing" (Hebrews 10:25), they say.

Anne shakes her head and sighs, "You have no idea how deeply I long to be gathered together with other Christians. The loneliness and isolation are almost unbearable."

Others say to her, "Stop looking for the *perfect* church."

Anne responds, "I'm not looking for a perfect church. I know I'll never find it. In fact, I want a church for broken, weak, and needy people, just like me. I know God's grace will be at work there."

We're all looking for a place of refuge where people are open to healing, honest about their pain, and willing to accept one another in the grace found at the Cross. Does God have such a place of rest, a place of sanctuary and safety for lonely hearts cut off from the world? Indeed, he created us to be in intimate relationship with one another. But the realities of life don't always shake out that way, and we're left with a pervading sense of aloneness.

Loneliness creates emotional refugees in a world packed full of people—some who are as lonely as we are. One church has pinpointed this dilemma in their community and prints these words in their Sunday bulletin along with a welcome invitation to be part of that church:

> Whatever happened to community? When our backyards were open and our neighborhoods were safe. When borrowing a cup of sugar might turn into an afternoon visit. When the best part of the day was not another video or a double-click on the mouse but quiet conversation over dinner. It seems in all our activity, we're missing togetherness. Oh, there are plenty of people around. Yet many of us are standing knee deep in a river dying of thirst. The walls around our homes are symbols of unseen walls around our hearts and community.[1]

Despite our social isolation, God invites us to come to an unhurried place where the heart is given special attention. Like a mother calling for her lost child, God gently calls us to enter his sanctuary of peace, where his presence gives us a reprieve from the dangers of physical, emotional, and spiritual loneliness.

Physical Loneliness

In a culture connected by cold, thin wires of technology and fragmented by the flurry of activity in our lives, God understands our physical loneliness when we live without true intimacy with others. He understands our longing for friends to wrap our arms around, or to hold our hands in prayer, or to greet with holy kisses (Romans 16:16). We need shoulders to lay our heads upon when we cry and warm bodies to sit next to us when we've just heard bad news.

Scripture is filled with individuals who experienced isolation, and Jesus always saw their need and sought to fill it. When he healed lepers, he often did it by touching them, because society had deemed them "untouchable." The bleeding woman, ostracized as "unclean," touched Jesus' robe to be healed. And after his death and resurrection, Jesus appeared to his grieving disciples and said, "It is I myself. Touch me and see" (Luke 24:39).

God's peace transcends our physical loneliness even on particularly tough days when we long for those friends who live in faraway places.

On almost a daily basis, God instills his peace in Anne through friends, acquaintances, even strangers at strategic times. She explains, "Frequently when I've become depressed because of feeling lonelier than usual, I've received two or three e-mail messages from friends—that same morning—usually followed by at least one phone call from a long-distance friend or family member.

"So I feel loved and valued not only by these people, but also by God, who hears my cries and continually provides this encouragement. It's not the same as physically participating in life with a committed community of believers, but God understands that need and is pointing me toward relationships with other believers." And in that direction lies our hope.

Emotional Loneliness

To feel lonely is to feel incomplete. Adam, in the midst of God's plenty in Eden, was overcome by the emotional loneliness he experienced as the only human. His emotional isolation was evidence that God had not yet completed his creation. He said, "It is not good for the man to be alone" (Genesis 2:18). What hope must have filled Adam when he heard God speak those words. God's intentional will that Adam not be alone gives us hope that he will supply our need for close relationships as well.

Hope implies a yearning for something better, a forward-thinking and forward-looking state of mind. But in the Christian world we often confuse hope with discontentment. After all, shouldn't we rejoice just to be loved by God and touched by his peace in our turmoil of loneliness? However, contentment does not mean an absence of longing. Proverbs says, "A longing fulfilled is sweet to the soul" (Proverbs 13:19).

Anne wrestles with this idea. When she considers the blessings in her life and the comforts that surround her, she believes most people would switch places with her in a heartbeat. And she struggles with wanting something more, occasionally wondering if it should be labeled "discontent."

"But God is the author of many of our desires and certainly the author of hope," Anne explains. "I believe he wants me to feel those longings and perhaps to agonize over them for a period of time, not shove them aside in a false sense of happiness." She's confident that God placed in her that need to connect with other people and with a church body. "He wants us to experience him through each other as well as on our own. Our loneliness is an alarm system that drives us to find others to be with. That's why I continue my search for a church home."

Understanding God's desire for her to be in community fills Anne with a hope that God himself renews in her each day. "The hope that he gave yesterday—no matter how personal and unique and specific—is not enough to get me through today," she says. "I sometimes feel embarrassed to come to him the very next day after he has generously given me a wonderful gift of hope. But I know that I need a *new* gift of hope, and that to try to hide that need from him would be dishonest." This is the only way to live in perfect peace—by focusing our thoughts and our longings on him every day (see Isaiah 26:3).

Jesus knew this truth when he told us to pray, "Give us *today* our daily bread" (Matthew 6:11, emphasis added). He knew that today's bread—emotional, spiritual, or physical—would be stale by tomorrow. It's the symbol of daily provision that God gave to the Israelites in their wilderness experience when he told them to gather enough manna to eat for one day only (Exodus 16:13–26). God expects us to gather in all the hope we need to meet today's emotional loneliness, and then ask again tomorrow, trusting him to provide at just the right time.

Spiritual Loneliness

When our prayers seemingly go unanswered and we begin to wonder if God is anywhere nearby, we may also experience a sense of spiritual loneliness. It happens even in the best of community life and friendships. That's when we cry out to God but fail to hear him answer. We perceive, in a very real sense, a separation from God, like darkness descending on a lost child at the end of the day. In the words of Emilie Griffin, "Trust and faith are the only companions for darkness, a walk that doesn't feel like a journey because there is no sense of going anywhere."[2]

As Anne cries out to God in her darkness, he reminds her of his faithfulness and his willingness to teach her to trust even when she senses she's going nowhere. "Part of the learning process has been in not receiving any clues from God about the future he plans for me—especially where I'll be or how soon," Anne says. God's peace in these times of darkness comes in direct proportion to our willingness to trust his goodness. But how can an invisible God come near to us and fill our need for physical contact? How can we truly experience the physical presence of a God who is spirit? Often it's through those individuals he sets in our path.

Anne's unceasing prayer has become "How long, Lord?" Such prayers put her in good company. Abraham received his promise to father a great nation, but had to wait at least fourteen years for the birth of his son Isaac. David was promised and anointed by God's prophet to be King of Israel, but waited in exile many years. In the meantime he ran for his life and lived in desolate caves until God's timing was right to fulfill his promise. The Psalms are filled with his laments and feelings of loneliness in the midst of God's promises.

Regardless of where we are on our spiritual journeys, whether traveling through loneliness or through community, we're in God's hands, within his divinely synchronized timetable. All he expects us to do is trust him to fulfill his promises and deliver us at just the right moment. Promises require trust. And in that combination we can live at peace with God and with ourselves.

Anne has grown accustomed to this road through loneliness and knows what to do when those extraordinary feelings thwart her most ordinary plans. There at her kitchen table, ready to eat her lunch, she stops, refocuses her mind on God, and once again tells him her need. She wipes away the tears and closes her eyes.

Her thoughts, moved by God's Spirit, take her to the foot of the cross. Holding her heavenly Father's hand, she hears him say, "Look at my Son. There is no one for whom he was more willing to die than for you. The purpose of his punishment was to bring you peace (Isaiah 53:5). If I love you that much, be assured, I'll never leave you." She takes in a deep breath of relief.

Although the aching loneliness lingers, the panic subsides as she rushes back to God's refuge of peace. In this sanctuary,

Anne continues her journey through loneliness, like the lost child always headed toward and hoping for a place to call home.

> *"How long, O Lord? Will you forget me forever? How long will you hide your face from me? How long must I wrestle with my thoughts and every day have sorrow in my heart? . . . But I trust in your un-failing love; my heart rejoices in your salvation. I will sing to the Lord, for he has been good to me"*

(Psalm 13:1–2, 5–6).

FACING LONELINESS

STUDY

Read the following narrative stories about people who may
have experienced loneliness: The woman at the well: John
4:4–26; Zacchaeus: Luke 19:1–10; Blind Bartimaeus:
Mark 10:46–52; John the Baptist in prison: Luke 7:18–23.

What circumstances contributed to their loneliness?

Meditate on how it would feel to live in their shoes.

How did Christ bring peace or reassurance of his presence
to these individuals?

CONSIDER

Loneliness is not a sin, only a human condition of the heart.
When and how have you experienced loneliness in your
life? In what way do you feel an incompleteness in your
life? Read Philippians 1:6 for reassurance that God will
not leave you in an incomplete state of being. How can
Christ instill peace in you while you live in this lonely
place?

PRAY

Cry out to God in your loneliness. Pour out your heartache
and your longing to him. Request a measure of peace to
descend on you today.

RESPOND

Thank him for his ability to comfort, provide, and come
alongside you in every way.

Read 2 Thessalonians 3:16 as your personal prayer.

Chapter Eight

SANCTUARY
OF
FAITHFULNESS

Sanctuary

They had argued about it for years. He never understood how it broke her heart or why his desire for pornography was destroying their marriage. Having grown up in a home where *Playboy* was kept in the magazine rack and where his dad often showed him the centerfold, it was hard for Dave to see it as a problem. The more Jenny confronted him on it, the harder he resisted. And the harder she defended her convictions, the greater the rift between them. Tired of arguing, she finally told God, "Enough." She knew her words held no power to change her husband, so she began to ask God to do it for her.

"I felt betrayed and belittled. Pornography was an act of adultery in my eyes. I knew it didn't fall within God's framework of marriage, so I was confident my prayers were within his will when I asked him to help Dave see the truth for himself. I even prayed that pornography would become repulsive to Dave. I asked God to make him sense the pain of his infidelity to me and our marriage vows. At the same time, I promised myself I'd stop haggling with Dave about it until

God made it clear to both of us that it was time to discuss it again."

As Jenny continued to pray for her husband, God also worked in her heart. She began to see her husband as a gift from God rather than a problem she needed to solve. She saw him as a wonderful provider, tenderhearted in so many ways, always helping others feel welcome and at ease. She thanked Dave for his acts of kindness and told him how much she appreciated his forthrightness in other areas of his life.

"But as I thanked God for the parts of my marriage that appeared as precious jewels, I also held up the part that I didn't understand, the part that appeared ugly. I asked, 'What is this, Lord?'" Like a child taking a broken treasure to her father to fix, Jenny held the unfaithfulness out to God to heal or to change or to explain how to deal with it.

Six months after she let go of trying to control the problem, things began to change. When Dave came home after work one evening, Jenny immediately knew something was wrong. She feared the worst, expecting him to say he was leaving her for another woman. Instead, he broke down and cried and admitted for the first time, "I have a problem and I'm out of control. Pornography has a grip on me and I want out of it. As hard as I try, I can't stop. I need someone to help me." The words continued to pour from his heart as fast as the tears fell. He confessed his sin not only to God but admitted it all to Jenny as well. He asked for her forgiveness as he cried over the possibility of *her* leaving him.

As difficult as Dave's confession was to listen to, all Jenny could hear was God answering her prayer, and she thanked him for his incredible work. Then she held Dave in her arms and promised to stay by him as they worked through the issues of sexual addiction and how it impacted their marriage.

Even if a marriage remains untouched by the extremes of sexual addiction, many individuals bring premarital sexual activity into the union. And illicit affairs are often shrugged off as "mistakes." But Jesus draws a much different picture of purity and marital faithfulness. His line defining adultery is not crossed with an act of infidelity, rather he draws the line straight through the heart, where adultery all begins. He said, "Anyone who looks at a woman lustfully has already committed adultery with her in his heart" (Matthew 5:26).

In a society where faithfulness is old-fashioned, we can almost hear promises shatter and marriage vows broken by the minute. Friends betray friends, families feud over trivialities, and loyalty depends on who's winning. As a result, we often don't know how to approach God's sanctuary of faithfulness. To many, God's faithfulness is as unfathomable as his omnipotence. We simply don't understand it or know what to expect there.

After Dave's confession to Jenny, they both expected the problem to diminish. But as with most addictive behaviors, eventually the old cycle of lust and desire, temptation and sin, returned with even greater force than before. Magazines weren't enough to feed his addiction; now Dave visited strip bars and even had an encounter with a prostitute. Certainly not the kind of result the couple expected after turning to God in repentance. Still, they never doubted his faithfulness to them as they both cried out for continued healing and help.

"I couldn't believe the life we were now living—AIDS

testing, addiction, infidelity, counseling, and support groups. Life seemed so unreal," Jenny says. But through it all, she continued to turn to God moment by moment. "He's never let me down as he's shown me over and over how he is faithful in so many ways."

Faithful to Uphold Honor

Jenny struggled with anger and resentment over Dave's actions. At one point, when she found out Dave was frequenting strip bars, she lashed out at him and said, "Do you have any idea how it makes me feel to know you're standing around someplace looking at another woman's body? It makes me feel like dirt!"

When a husband chooses to feast his eyes on other women, a wife's sense of beauty and self-worth can quickly fade. Even the "innocent" double take at the attractive woman at a nearby table can begin a destructive process in the mind. That's why the line of purity in marriage is drawn so close to the heart. God must have known the pain of such feelings, because Scripture is filled with words intended to restore honor to those who are being destroyed by the lies of the world.

Infidelity may knock us down and degrade our sense of beauty, but God surrounds us with a wall of love and acceptance. Like a secret garden, he hedges us in with his faithfulness and replaces the lies and distortions about our beauty with rich promises and pictures of honor. There we can regain our footing and stand strong when we hear his words: "I will give you the treasures of darkness, riches stored in secret places. . . . I summon you by name and bestow on you a title of honor" (Isaiah 45:3–4).

Jenny frequently battles self-doubt, wondering what she could have done or not done to have kept Dave faithful in their marriage. At such times she's learned to immediately turn to God through Scripture for his reassurance of her worth. "As long as I'm living for him, he's always faithful to protect and defend my honor."

Like a great champion, God has preserved her sense of completeness with words like these: "Do not be afraid; you will not suffer shame. Do not fear disgrace; you will not be humiliated. . . . For your Maker is your husband—the Lord Almighty is his name. . . . I will build you with stones of turquoise, your foundations with sapphires. I will make your battlements of rubies, your gates of sparkling jewels, and all your walls of precious stones" (Isaiah 54:4–5, 11–12).

When we understand that our only source of true beauty and honor emanate from our Creator rather than from any outside opinion or influence (even from a spouse), then we're free to continue loving ourselves and loving one another more fully. It's this attitude that's taken unneeded pressure off Dave and Jenny. "I don't have to wait for Dave to say the right thing or do the right thing in order to feel valued. Certainly his words and actions have the ability to build me up just as my words can build him up, but we're learning to look beyond what we expect from each other and look to God as our source of strength and encouragement and honor."

Faithful to Forgive

People who know about Dave and Jenny's situation wonder how they stay together. In the case of infidelity, even

Scripture gives us an out from such a marriage (Matthew 19:9). "I do sometimes wonder if I'm not like the women who are abused over and over but refuse to save themselves. They continue to enable the behavior by staying," Jenny says. But she works hard to hold the standard high, to expect the best from Dave, and to expect honesty in their marriage. "When I'm feeling frightened or angry, I tell Dave. When he's feeling tempted or has somehow fallen, we talk about it.

"In one sense, I'm able to remain level-headed and un-emotional, better able to play a support role, when I remind myself this isn't about me, it's about Dave's addiction. But in another sense, when two people are joined in marriage, they become one. So in a very real way it's my problem, too, and it certainly touches me in many realms of my life. But when people wonder how we manage to stay together, let alone have a vital relationship, I tell them it's grace."

Indeed, grace seems to be synonymous with marriage. Even in ideal circumstances, the marriage relationship requires a continual laying down of our lives to each other and to God, imploring his mercy. Jenny says, "I'm as much of a sinner as Dave, and I'm in constant need of grace as well. There have been times when I've shut down emotionally or physically to protect my hurting heart, and I've turned away from Dave. Isn't that also an act of unfaithfulness on my part?" If two people approach each other in grace, expecting to give it and receive it, and together they come to God, then it's possible to experience an ever deepening relationship even in the darkest situation.

Forgiveness is a huge part of God's sanctuary of faithfulness, for he says, "If we confess our sins, he is *faithful* and just and will forgive us our sins and purify us from all un-righteousness" (1 John 1:9, emphasis added).

Faithful to Redeem

Redemption is the hope we hold on to in the midst of an unfaithful world. Redemption is the act of relinquishing something of little value and receiving something of great value in return. When we fail to live up to our commitments in relationships, all we can hope for is an act of redemption that allows us to start over again. But God's faithfulness goes beyond even that. His faithfulness doesn't stop at "Let's start over." He goes back to where we've already started and failed and actually makes something good and worthwhile happen through it. All we need to do is willingly turn it over to him. "And we know that in all things God works for the good of those who love him" (Romans 8:28).

What good is there in sexual addiction and unfaithful-ness? None. When is an affair or a lustful look a good thing? Never. But when we humbly turn to God with what we have of little value, he exchanges it for something of great value—his faithfulness. In that process our lives become a living tes-timony of God's work of love in an unfaithful world, a pic-ture of forgiveness and redemption. And that picture has the potential to put others in a place to receive God's grace as well and to live within his sanctuary of faithfulness.

Jenny continues to look for God's good work in the midst of the disappointments in her marriage. "Sexual infi-delity is a very private pain. Most people aren't willing to admit it, let alone share it with the world. But in being open about it with each other and even with close friends and within our church body, we've seen many doors open up for healing in other lives, as well. I hope it's eased the burden that someone may have carried alone for so long. This struggle has probably given us a depth in our relationship we never would have known before, a complete vulnerability that some marriages lack. I'm not saying everyone should experience it or that this is great for a marriage. It has definitely left unwanted scars on our relationship. But I continue to remind myself that even Jesus has scars from this life. And look at the good that produced for all of us."

Today Dave continues to work out with God this problem of sexual addiction. Pornography no longer controls his life, but at times he struggles with the temptation. And Jenny continues to pray for complete restoration of their marriage and her sense of value. There will always be a continual building and rebuilding of their relationship. But in God's sanctuary they rejoice, because hidden in a secret garden of faithfulness, he surrounds them with the beauty of honor, forgiveness, and redemption.

"I will betroth you to me forever; I will betroth you in righteousness and justice, in love and compassion. I will betroth you in faithfulness, and you will acknowledge the Lord"

(Hosea 2:19–20).

STANDING ON SOLID GROUND

STUDY

Read Psalm 91:4. List the ways God's faithfulness protects you. (A rampart can be defined in several ways: an army, a defender, a protective barrier, a broad embankment raised as fortification.)

Compare that definition of faithfulness to the picture of being covered with the softness of feathers.

How do both descriptions apply to God's faithfulness to you in an unfaithful world?

Read Hosea 2:20. According to this verse we respond to God's promise of faithfulness by acknowledging him as Lord. How does this differ from our inability to always *feel* God's faithfulness?

CONSIDER

Of the three areas of faithfulness discussed in this chapter (honor, forgiveness, redemption), which is the most difficult for you to experience? What keeps you from knowing this facet of God's love? Ask him how you can more fully move into his sanctuary in every aspect of life.

PRAY

Acknowledge God's faithfulness. Recognize his goodness as solid fact. Praise him that he's given you a firm place to stand. Acknowledge the ways he's been faithful to you today and in the past. Confess to him any areas where you have been unfaithful to him or in your relationships.

RESPOND

If marital unfaithfulness has affected your life in any way, determine not to carry the burden as a "private pain."

Ask God to help you find another woman strong in the faith to talk with. Seek her counsel and ask her to bear that burden with you and pray with you.

Chapter Nine

SANCTUARY
OF
DELIVERANCE

Sanctuary

From the outside, they looked like a typical family. Twelve-year-old Laurel walked to school with her older sister and younger brother. She even waved to neighbors on the way down the street. But deep down, she wondered, *Did anyone hear? Did they hear my daddy threatening to kill us all night long because of the bad grade I made at school? Did they hear Mom tell me that it would be my fault if Daddy went to hell?*

In one breath she prayed nobody had heard. But by the time she exhaled she prayed somebody would hear and do something about it. Laurel's mother and father both came from a long line of alcoholic, abusive families. "Mother dealt with life through denial and control. She always pretended we were a normal, happy little family and that she was an ordinary housewife like all the other women on the block and at church."

Beyond the unpredictable and raging threats of death, Laurel's father was also a deceitful man, a con artist who swindled dozens of people out of thousands of dollars. Law enforcement officers frequently knocked at their door or watched and waited in unmarked cars down the street. And if it wasn't the cops or the FBI who came calling, it was someone Dad had swindled.

Heavy drapes covered every window, sequestering the family from the world and from any hope of deliverance. The children were rarely allowed to answer the phone or the door. "I do remember answering the phone one time," Laurel says. "The man on the other end said, 'Tell your daddy that I'm gonna chop his little girl into pieces if he doesn't pay up.'" For years thereafter the phone terrified Laurel.

"If the doorbell rang, we all froze or were told to drop down to the floor. Daddy hid guns all over the house because of the dozens of break-ins that occurred." Many nights the sound of a cocking gun or someone trying to break through the front door woke Laurel.

During her childhood, Laurel's father was in and out of prison. Other times he went to live with girlfriends or "business partners." As a result of his long absences, and despite the money he'd stolen, the family often lived in poverty, with no running water or electricity for weeks at a time. Usually someone from the local church paid to have the electricity turned back on.

Laurel's mom started taking her children to church when they were quite young. Laurel immediately fell in love with Jesus. "I asked Christ into my life at a young age. I truly knew who he was and what I was doing. But more importantly, God also knew what he was doing because he spared my life over and over again throughout my growing-up years."

For instance, when Laurel was eight, she saw no other

way to cope with her torturous homelife, so she tried to kill herself by drinking poison. Somehow she survived. Shortly after that incident, she had a vision one night of an angel. "It was so real. The angel told me, 'Don't be afraid any more because God is with you and will always be with you'" (Psalm 34:7).

Laurel believes God allowed that angel or the dream of that angel to give her the strength and courage to face the struggles she would confront in the days ahead. Never again did she attempt to take her own life despite a harrowing childhood of poverty, unwarranted beatings, death threats, sexual molestation, and forced exploitation in pornographic films.

Still she continued to wonder if anyone knew or cared about her suffering. As she waved to the neighbors on her way to school, she dreamed of what it would be like if someone came to deliver them all from this wide-awake nightmare going on behind closed doors.

Abuse does strange things to a mind, especially one as moldable as a child's. "I developed several mechanisms to cope with the conflict," Laurel explains. "I thought if I tried to be good, life would be better for everyone. But when compliant good behavior failed to stop the abuse, I rebelled and became full of raging anger. I felt ugly and dirty and unworthy. After I was out on my own, I lived a promiscuous life for several years." But Laurel's chaotic choices and emotions kept her disengaged from life and hidden behind a heavy veil of fear.

With each failure to find answers and satisfactory methods of handling her hurt, she found God living up to his promise to always be with her. Over and over again, he extended his strong hand to pull her out of the mess and into his sanctuary of deliverance.

Deliverance From Anger

Forgiving the wrongs inflicted on us doesn't happen overnight, especially when our hearts become saturated with anger toward the wrongdoers. After a year of counseling, and with the support of godly men and women in her church, Laurel came to the conclusion that obedience to God would play the strongest role in her healing process. It freed her to forgive her offenders even when they failed to acknowledge their part in the abuse or to ask for forgiveness.

The surprising thing is that her ability to forgive has come about only as she's been willing to recognize her own sin and receive God's forgiveness. "My anger and rebellion, my inability to honor my parents, all these were areas of sin that I held toward those who had hurt me. My sin hindered my healing."

The first step toward deliverance has to be a desire to look at ourselves and the areas we need to deal with, not what others have done to us. "I look back and regret the wasted years where I longed for and hoped for others to repent. Then I burned with anger when I didn't see it happen. It took a long time to understand that God was waiting for me to turn to him and seek his heart and his forgiveness. I thought I would be freed if and when others were broken or changed, but I've found that I was freed when I was broken and contrite over my own sin" (Isaiah 57:15).

Over time, Laurel has tried to reach out to her parents. After years of no contact with her father, she had a brief encounter with him when he made it clear he wanted no part in mending past hurts or healing their relationship. Her mother has turned her back on the church and on God, believing instead that she can create happiness on her own. She refuses to acknowledge any hurtful actions toward her children. Laurel prays for her mother and father even as she continues the process of learning to forgive day by day.

Deliverance From Rebellion

When Laurel moved out of her childhood home, she took with her an attitude of rebellion against her parents. Resentment drew another heavy drape over her life, separating her from her parents. She vehemently promised herself never to treat her children like she'd been treated, never to be like her parents, never to be poor, and never to marry someone like her father.

But those vows also kept her from fully entering God's sanctuary. As she grew in the Lord, she realized that as right as her vows sounded, they emerged from the sin of rebellion. "When I realized what I was doing, I began asking the Lord to instill in me his thoughts, his precepts, his ways, and that whatever decisions or vows I made, he be the author of them."

This redirection in her attitude required what Laurel calls a two-step act of obedience. First, it required she obey with her will: "I obey because God wants me to and because I love him. I don't necessarily have the feelings needed to do what he asks. I may even feel angry or rebellious or even full of revenge on certain days, but with my will I obey."

That leads to the second step: heart obedience. "This is a natural outflow of my heart, which has been trained by willful obedience. In this second step, I realize I obey God because I want to, because I can't help myself. The more I follow step one, the more my heart begins to change in step two."

Ultimately, Laurel renounced her rebellious vows "against her parents" and asked God to rewrite those areas and imprint them with his desires. In fact, God has allowed her to keep all her original promises. But the sweet blessing is that the vows have been carried out because of the work of Christ in her, not because of her rebellion.

Deliverance From Oppression

Having lived through an abusive childhood, the tapes that played in Laurel's head oppressed her and kept her bound to the lies of the world: "You're rotten"; "You're ugly"; "You'll never amount to anything"; "You're stupid." Even if such insults were never spoken, the years of emotional, physical, and sexual abuse pounded the attitudes into her head.

But God's Word and his message of love are stronger than those oppressive thoughts. "You, dear children, are from God and have overcome them, because the one who is in you [Christ] is greater than the one who is in the world" (1 John 4:4). Through prayer and meditation, God promises to regroove the way we see things. "Do not conform any longer to the pattern of this world, but be transformed by the renewing of your mind" (Romans 12:2).

Often when we read Scripture so contrary to our "tapes" recorded at childhood, we find it hard to connect to the reality of God's thoughts. But we can quicken this process of deliverance from oppression by literally calling on the name of Jesus. There is no other name given to us that is able to save (Acts 4:12).

Consider, too, God's name revealed to Moses at the burning bush: "I AM." Perhaps God gave us this saving name for two reasons: First, I AM covers every need. For Moses it covered his lack of authority, his lack of confidence, his lack of credentials, and even his lack of desire to do God's will. God, in essence, was saying, "It doesn't matter what you lack, because I AM . . . all that you aren't."

When we consider God as the great I AM, he's giving us the opportunity to fill in the blank, to allow us to turn over the tapes. For example, when the tape says, "I'm ugly," his name says, "I AM . . . your beauty" (Psalm 27:4). When we hear, "I'll never amount to anything," he says, "I AM . . . your everything" (Colossians 1:15–20).

Second, I AM is present tense. It's here and now. We can always look back to see the signposts of where God has been in our lives, and we can look forward with the hope and knowledge that he will fulfill his promises to us. But what a comfort to know that he comes alongside us right now: always present, always available, every moment, every day. All our deliverance from oppression is wrapped up God's name: I AM.

Deliverance From Being Good Enough

When Laurel was twenty-six years old she struggled with releasing a control tactic that she used to ease her pain. She tried to "be good," to please all the people all the time. But, of course, the harder we try to be good, the more energy and strength and willpower it saps from us until we're worn down to a bare-bone existence and cry out in our weariness, "I can't do it anymore! I'm not good enough!" One afternoon God spoke to Laurel about her final stronghold of resistance to his deliverance.

After a particularly stressful day, Laurel came home from work, ran inside the house, and told her children she needed to be alone with God for a few minutes. Then she went into her bedroom and flung herself on the bed and cried out to God. "I'm trying so hard to be good enough for you, good enough for my family, and good enough for my friends. I'm trying *so* hard."

Then Laurel heard the only words she *never* wanted to hear God say: "Laurel, you're not good enough!" Did she hear right? He said it again. "You're not good enough." Then, once more: "Laurel, you're not good enough . . . but no one is. That's why I sent my Son. He is the only one who is good enough."

"At that moment, I saw not only my own brokenness but precisely why Christ died for me. I was set free in a way that I never knew was possible. God delivered me from my desire to please everyone, to be the best, to earn the approval of others . . . it was gone, taken, lifted away." When Christ becomes our salvation and deliverer, we no longer bear the burden of being good enough to earn God's love, or anyone else's. He's done that job for us on the Cross. *He is good enough.*

Centuries ago a heavy drape literally hung between God and humanity in the temple. Once each year a purified priest entered into God's presence behind the curtain, the Holy of Holies, to sprinkle a blood sacrifice as payment for the sins of the people. But Jesus, our perfect, all-sufficient sacrifice, broke through the separation on our behalf. At the moment of his death, God tore the veil in the temple that sequestered us from our Deliverer (Mark 15:38). And with that tearing, we are able to enter into the Holy of Holies, the inner sanctuary where God dwells.

Today many who live through traumatic circumstances call themselves victims or survivors. Laurel has a different idea, because she no longer has to imagine what it would be like for someone to hear her call for help and rescue her from the pain. She knows her Deliverer and gladly inhabits that place of safety. "I've rejected the labels of victim and survivor. I can say instead, 'I am a *thriver* through Jesus Christ my Lord.'"

> *"I sought the Lord, and he answered me; he delivered me from all my fears. Those who look to him are radiant; their faces are never covered with shame"*

(Psalm 34:4–5).

Claiming the Name of God

Study

In Scripture, God reveals himself through hundreds of different names and forms. Read Isaiah 9:6 for several names in one verse. Consider what each of these names means to you.

Why has God given us so many different names to call upon?

Isaiah 7:14 calls Jesus "Immanuel," which means "God with us." How has God been with you in recent days?

Describe how you know him better because of the realization that he is always near you.

Consider

In the Old Testament, whenever God was with someone, they often called him by a new name based on their experience with him. What new name can you call him based on your awareness of him in your life? Is he the God of the Pocketbook when you can't pay the rent or the King of Rest and Restoration when you can't sleep? Be creative as you worship his name, the God of all Creation.

Pray

As you spend time in God's Word this week, be especially aware of the names that reveal God's personality. Jot down one or two names to focus on throughout your day. Write them on 3 × 5 cards to keep nearby. Call on those names as you go about your routines and ask him to make his name real for you. Simply whisper his name as a prayer.

RESPOND

Begin a journal to record your personal discoveries and Scripture discoveries of God's names.

Write down the circumstances surrounding your discovery. You'll soon have a journal full of God's treasures and you'll know him so much more intimately as a result.

Chapter Ten

SANCTUARY
OF
LOVE

When Sue was five years old, her great-grandpa died. The night of his death, she sat on the front porch to contemplate the big questions of life. Her mother came and sat next to her, and together they looked at the stars. But the sky, so big and black, offered no comfort. Sue turned instead to her mother and asked, "What happens when we die, Mommy?"

A moment of silence passed. Finally her mother drew in a breath and said flatly, "Nothing. You die and you're dead. Death is death." At that moment, those words cut a hole in Sue's soul as deep and dark as the night sky overhead, except without the stars. It left her feeling more frightened than ever before. But all she could do was what any five-year-old would naturally do. She simply trusted and accepted her mother's words as the terrible truth.

The dark void created from that conversation grew like a black hole in space collapsing in on itself, at times devouring the life and light out of anything that came near it. In Sue's home, no one ever talked about God, religion, or beliefs about life or death. Her father, a workaholic, traveled for days at a time. Her mother, trying to be both mom and dad to five children, simply didn't have the time or the energy to consider such questions.

So Sue held her thoughts inside, hoping the black hole wouldn't consume all the joy of living. "If I thought about dying, or was confronted by death in any way, I would be physically sick and cry out of control, sometimes for hours, because I thought, *That's it. There is no more after I die.* It made me physically ill in the pit of my stomach."

A feeling of panic followed her even into adulthood. She stayed as far away from the edge of that consuming fear as possible. She even steered clear of God, assuming he had something to do with the dark hole in her heart. So she drifted through her growing-up years with no concept of God other than a fear of the unknown.

The big questions of life eventually confronted her again, in a surprising way, during her wedding. Neither she nor her fiancé, Eric, were Christians, although they had a "church" ceremony. She remembers the minister saying, *"Marriage is one of the important steps of life, like being born and dying."* Although they later laughed it off as a joke, it planted a tiny thought within her: *What is the point to life if there's nothing at the end?* The mere whisper of an idea about life and death sent a shiver of fear through her soul once again.

Fear comes in all shapes and sizes, colors and textures. A nameless man in the Bible was tormented with myriad fears called evil spirits or demons. They plagued and hounded him until he lived like a wild man among the tombs. When Jesus met him, he spoke directly to the demon and asked, "What is your name?" The demon answered, "Legion, for we are many" (Mark 5:1–20).

We, too, can be tortured by fears, and sometimes, as in Sue's life, they come in "legion" proportions. Today we may not call them demons, but we know fear by many names—failure, the future, rejection, pain, death, and a host of other tormentors. If we allow those fears to take up residence in us, they try to control us in every way.

We open the door to fear with the key of worry. We believe that if we worry hard enough or long enough things will change. But rather than shed light on the problem, worry expands the darkness. It can turn our hearts black with panic, leaving us physically shaky, short of breath, and crying for hours. But there is a way out of the darkness. The only means of banishing the blackness lies in the name of love.

No one has ever fully defined love. But love is fully embodied in the name and person of God. God is love (1 John 4:16). And love never ends (1 Corinthians 13:8 NRSV). And so we come to God's sanctuary of love. This sanctuary differs from the others because it's already built inside us, but it lies empty and dormant like that black hole of fear. In order to turn this space into God's sanctuary—into our safe place to dwell—we need to invite him in to occupy it and fill it with his light and love.

Until we take that step, he stands outside and politely knocks on the door. He waits for us to put our hand to the knob. He listens for the latch to click. He watches for the door to open. And he waits for our words of welcome, inviting him in. His gently pursuing love longs to change us from the inside out as he shines his light into that dark space of fear.

God's Love Woos Our Hearts

God's love is patient and waits for us to respond to him by returning his love. "I have loved you with an everlasting love; I have drawn you with loving kindness" (Jeremiah 31:3). He loved us before we ever loved him (1 John 4:19).

Sue can look back on her life now and see how gently God drew her with loving-kindness and prepared a path for her to walk. Ten years after their marriage, Sue and Eric moved with their two young children from the East Coast to Arizona hoping for a relaxed lifestyle and milder climate. But with no job for the first several months after their move, they quickly found themselves deep in debt with no plan for ever getting out. Their lifestyle was anything but relaxing as their financial brokenness put great strains on their relationship and great needs in their lives. They began to wonder if the move had been a big mistake.

But when Eric finally found work, he also gained a co-worker, a Christian, who invited him to church. Eric knew how Sue would react to church. She had said it a dozen times before: "Why would I want to get up early on a Sunday morning and ruin a perfectly good day with church?" So he made excuses to be out of the house on Sunday mornings and "secretly" began to attend church with his new friend. When Eric finally admitted his Sunday destination, Sue shrugged but heard another whisper daring her to hope for a change in their life situation.

Shortly thereafter a flier came in the mail about a new church nearby. She agreed to check it out. The first series of messages were about family life and marriage. It spoke to Sue in a powerful way. It addressed their family problems, their relationship, and the needs in their everyday life. "It seemed God wanted us in a place of brokenness to get our attention. I wondered if the pastor had been to our house. It was eerie how precisely his sermons hit home. I had no choice but to pay attention to the message and listen to what God was saying about my life." It was another aspect of God's love patiently courting her heart.

God's Love Waits for an Open Door

In an attempt to deal with the pain and fear of dying, Sue had contrived her own concepts about God and life after death. "I had decided that if there was a God he had to be loving and would certainly understand my upbringing and allow me to live with him. I just didn't know I had a choice in the matter. It was simply the way I figured God would be."

But like any loving creature, God doesn't force his love on us nor does he demand we love him in return. His heart continually pursues us but never intrudes on us. All he desires is for us to open the door to invite him in by recognizing Jesus as the only way into that relationship. "Listen! I am standing at the door, knocking; if you hear my voice and open the door, I will come in to you and eat with you, and you with me" (Revelation 3:20 NRSV).

Sue opened that door nine months after first setting foot

inside the church. In a quiet moment alone, she invited Christ into her heart. There was no fanfare or hoopla, no "hallelujah" or "praise the Lord." She didn't even entirely know what it would mean in the end. But she knew she could no longer deny God's love drawing her to his side, nor could she live without him in her life.

God's Love Delights in Us

When we so desperately seek a Savior and a safe place to dwell, we often forget that our choice to enter God's sanctuary gives him great pleasure, as well. "The Lord your God is with you, he is mighty to save. He will take great delight in you, he will quiet you with his love, he will rejoice over you with singing" (Zephaniah 3:17).

During those first few months in church, Sue felt God's love woo her. And when she and Eric decided to be baptized, a new dimension of joy descended on her as she understood Christ's delight in her decision. There beside the backyard pool where she would be immersed, a large wooden cross had been erected in the dirt. The pastor handed her a slip of paper with her name written on it. Then he held out a hammer and a nail.

"I knew what I had to do, what God wanted me to do. I remember thinking, *I have to be right there, in his hand.* So I nailed my name where Jesus' right hand would have been on the cross. That's where I knew he wanted me to be. My full devotion came at that moment." One of Sue's favorite verses reminds her of that moment of mutual delight in realizing she was bonded to Christ as together they hold on to each other. "My soul clings to you; your right hand upholds me" (Psalm 63:8).

God's Love Casts Out Any Fear

Once we've invited Christ into our lives, his love is ready and willing to protect us from evil and fear when we choose to rest in him. "Perfect love drives out fear" (1 John 4:18). This truth doesn't stem from our own ability to love perfectly. In fact, we simply don't have the human capacity to love "perfectly" or completely. Only God can do that. In other words, when we allow God to love us completely through his Son, he drives away our deepest fears and destroys them.

"I no longer float through life hoping I don't get consumed by this black hole inside me. I now have a place to put my fear and the sense of foreboding I'd lived with for so long." The man possessed by the "legion" of demons walked among the tombs night and day and cried out in his torment . . . until he met Jesus. That encounter with the Savior changed him. It restored him to his right mind. He was ready to follow Christ and to tell others how much Christ had done for him.

When Sue met Jesus, she no longer cried out at her fear hidden in the tombs of death. Her encounter with the Savior destroyed the tormenting thoughts of eternal darkness and separation from God. He turned that dark and empty space into his sanctuary, and she's never again panicked at the thought of death. Even facing death in her own family, she's found peace rather than panic. She can picture the beauty of heaven and what it will be like to see God's face, to walk with him and hold his right hand.

"See, the home of God is among mortals. He will dwell with them; they will be his peoples, and God himself will be with them; he will wipe every tear from their eyes. Death will be no more; mourning and crying and pain will be no more, for the first things have passed away" (Revelation 21:3–4 NRSV).

Sue was partially right in her assumptions of long ago. God does have something to do with the black hole as dark as the midnight sky. He's the one who destroys it and reassures us that there is a point to living and something wonderful after this life is done. In the end there is love, and love never ends.

"For great is your love toward me; you have delivered me from the depths of the grave"

(Psalm 86:13).

PERFECTING LOVE

STUDY

Read 1 Corinthians 13:1–13. Why do you think a lack of love invalidates spiritual gifts and acts of service? (vv. 1–3)

Verses 4–6 give a descriptive list of love in action. How does this differ from *feelings* of love?

Out of this list of actions, which is the most difficult for you to perfect?

Using the list in verses 4–6, how did God reveal himself in those ways in Sue's story? How has he shown his love to you?

Verse 12 talks about our lack of clear vision in this life. How can God's love change the way we view life?

CONSIDER

On page 133 it says, "We open the door to fear with the key of worry." What are the things you worry about? What do you see as the underlying fear to these concerns? Do you believe God cares about your worries? Read 1 Peter 5:7 for reassurance.

PRAY

With your palms open before God, release each worry to him. Ask him to replace your anxiety and deep-down fear with his love and peace. Read Philippians 4:6–7 and turn it into your personal prayer.

RESPOND

Using this same verse, write down how you believe God would personally speak these words to you.

Use this during the week as your reminder of God's multi-faceted love that drives away fear.

Epilogue

How can words express the heart of God? How can a writer describe the glory of God's presence or his holy sanctuary? Even his name, in Hebrew, is an unspeakable, unknowable essence of beauty. No human this side of heaven has ever looked upon his brilliance and lived. So how do we dare attempt to convey the character of almighty Jehovah?

God himself reassures us that there is a way. It's the same way he chose to reveal himself to us—within a human life. God expressed his Word, his very thoughts, by allowing them to become flesh in the form of Jesus (John 1:1, 14). Through Christ, we, too, are given the holy privilege of revealing God to the world through the gift of life. For *we* hold this treasure in jars of clay (2 Corinthians 4:7, emphasis added).

God has chosen human life as the perfect vessel for displaying his countenance and character because only a living being can be transformed from dust to dignity. When we see such a person, we don't say, "What a great or courageous person you are." Rather, we can exclaim, "What an amazing God you must know!" Human life becomes evidence for and testimony to the richness of this righteous God.

But still we wonder how. Our lives often appear as a rubble of ruins, and we wonder why God would choose to inhabit such a mess in the first place? Perhaps one of the most vivid pictures of God's desire and love for us is seen in the bell ringer Quasimodo. This Christ-figure, who rescued Esmerelda, brought her into the Notre Dame Cathedral and cried out in victory, "Sanctuary! Sanctuary!"

But even as Esmerelda entered that safe place, harbored from certain death, she brought with her doubts and fears about being there. Still, her savior continued to tenderly provide for her every need. He never forced his love on her, but waited patiently for her to turn to him and look at him and behold his heart of beauty as he held out to her new garments—a white robe and a veil.

> Scarcely had she finished dressing, when she saw Quasimodo returning. He was carrying a basket under one arm and a mattress under the other. The basket held a bottle, some bread, and other provisions. He put it on the ground and said to her, "Eat." He placed the mattress on the flagstone, and said, "Sleep." It was his own meal, his own bed, that the bell ringer had gone to fetch. . . .
>
> At the same time, as if some invisible hand had lifted the weight that had so long kept her tears within her, she began to weep; and as the tears flowed, she felt the sharpest and bitterest of her grief washing away with them. . . .
>
> So in this place of sanctuary, hope returned to her. . . . The terrible images that so long haunted her began to withdraw gradually. . . . For love is like a tree; it grows of itself; it sends its roots deep into our being and often continues to grow green over a heart in ruins.[1]

If your heart lies in ruins, come to this hiding place where hope returns and love runs deep. If you carry a heavy burden, come rest in this safe dwelling and accept the gifts God lays at your feet. If you have nowhere else to turn, then let him cry out for you, "Sanctuary!" Then run to his open arms and proclaim, "I'm home free!"

May you always dwell richly in the sanctuary of God, the only safe place for your soul.

SMALL GROUP NOTES

When I began talking to women about their stories of sanctuary, an interesting thing happened. I became more and more open with my own struggles and aware of my need for God's sanctuary, as well. I also realized what a blessing I'd been given to work through those struggles with the insight of these women. Their courage in putting their lives "in print" for the sake of helping others strengthened me when I felt weary in the work.

These women revealed themselves in a most vulnerable way. Consequently, Christ revealed his power in a most perfect way—through their weaknesses. No one told their story without shedding tears. No one shared without some trepidation. Each one prayed for God's leading in opening up her heart to the world. I share these thoughts with you in the hope that they will help you and your friends to find that same safe place with each other—as you grow together and share your own stories of sanctuary in your walk with God.

I encourage you to use the following suggestions to make your discussion and the environment where you meet a "safe place" for each woman. Many will be fearful of uncovering long-festering heart-wounds. Some may choose not to become vulnerable. Your attitude will help instill confidence in others that your time together is God's invitation into his sanctuary.

Before you arrive each week, ask God to make each woman tenderhearted toward one another. Ask him to prepare your minds for new understanding and insight into his personality.

When you come together, do not begin the study until you've discussed the following concerns:

Confidentiality: While women are encouraged to share general concepts, teachings, and new insights with others outside your group, it is critical that personal sharing of lives is kept in confidence and does not leave the room where you meet. This is the emotional safety net we hold out to each other as we fall into the safe place of God's arms. The more honest and open you are with each other (and you may need to lead the way and be willing to share your heart first), the more open they will be to receive God's healing and to grow in him.

Commitment: Commit to meet in the same place and time each week. Commit to faithful attendance. This solidifies the group and helps create trust even beyond your meeting time. Women will know they can depend on each other. Commit to pray for one another at least once during the week. Make every effort to prepare and study ahead of time. The best discussion is based on the discovery process through study during the week.

Covenant: Either in writing or verbally, covenant with one another to honor the confidentiality and the commitment, in an effort to truly understand our place of sanctuary.

Study Notes

The following notes don't give specific answers to questions, because most of the study questions are based in self-discovery. This is simply a place to offer suggestions and prompt thoughts into the subject and to prepare you for possible issues being discussed. The study questions at the end of each chapter usually deal with one small aspect of the material in the chapter. Feel free to choose another aspect from your reading to develop in your discussion time.

Most of the questions and exercises are self-explanatory. Simply ask your group to share new insights or ongoing struggles related to these areas. Also, reflect as a group on the story of the woman in the chapter, how you relate to her, differ from her, etc. You will also note that many of the Scriptures mentioned do not appear in written form in the chapter text. The more you open God's Word and review these Scriptures, the more God will speak to your heart.

Chapter 1—Sanctuary of Grace

1 John 1:9. Confession and conversion is an ongoing, everyday process. We can't know God's grace on a daily basis without also acknowledging our need for it. Discuss ways of practicing confession on a daily basis. If women have difficulty recalling sin in their lives, encourage them to seek God's counsel. Ask him to uncover the sin as a means to opening the door of sanctuary.

Psalm 103:10–13. Some women may wonder why they continue to feel burdened by guilt when this passage says that God has removed our sins from us. Remind them that often our memories protect us from the same mistakes. Even David said, "My sin is always before me" (Psalm 51:3). We see the brilliance of God's grace shining like diamonds against the dark backdrop of our sin. However, God does not want us to be bound by past sins when we can walk in freedom. (This will be discussed further in chapter 9—Sanctuary of Deliverance.)

Ephesians 1:7–10. This passage refers to different aspects of God's grace, such as giving us his wisdom and understanding, revealing his will and desire to us, and instilling a hope for an eternal future ("when the times will have reached their fulfillment"). Ask for specific examples of how God's grace has impacted the women in your group. This would also be a good time to discuss the list of people who have extended grace to them. What new insights into grace did they discover in this exercise?

Chapter 2—Sanctuary of Comfort

Hebrews 4:12. This passage says that the Word of God penetrates and divides in the following ways. Ask the women to give specific examples of what would fall within each of these areas of life. Some examples are given.

Soul and spirit (spiritual life)—God's grace, our sin, holiness, confession, prayer, etc.

Joints and marrow (physical life)—outward actions, eating, rest, sex, work, dealing with pain, illness, life, death, morality, etc.

Thoughts and attitudes (intellectual and emotional life)—

thought life, education, judgments, prejudice, selfishness, compassion, servanthood, resentment, anger, etc.

When the Word of God "divides" these areas, it separates the natural tendencies from godly ones, discerns any inconsistency between our thoughts and God's, and enables us to weed out what doesn't please God. Nothing is excluded from the power of the Word.

John 1:1–5, 14. The *Word* comes from a Greek word that means *thought*—God's thoughts made flesh. Just as at Creation he formed life with a mere spoken word, so, too, "the Word made flesh" reveals a new creation. Although Jesus existed with and within the Father, God's ability to bring this reality to us in the flesh was both an act of his mighty power and his amazing grace. It expressed his desire to be with us and comfort us like no other act since the creation of the world. Discuss how Christ has changed the lives of the women in the group as well as how he has changed our world.

Chapter 3—Sanctuary of Acceptance

Isaiah 30:15–16. This is a study in contrast between God's sanctuary and our rebellion. He offers quietness, rest, and an unburdening of our heavy hearts. But to grab hold of his gift means we have to slow down . . . stop . . . and turn to God. Compare that place of rest to the picture in verse 16 and the speed at which we live our lives today. Even our "pursuers" chase us down in a wild horse race.

Discuss what things or situations chase us away from God's quiet sanctuary. Why do we choose to get on those horses and run away? How might our busy lifestyle be an act of rebellion toward God? This does not mean God isn't with us when life gets busy. It only means there is more competing for our attention—competing with God for our attention. It makes it more difficult to sense God's presence and to hear his thoughts guiding us when his sanctuary is being drowned out by schedules, calendars, and to-do lists.

Chapter 4—Sanctuary of Truth

Although we often fear our weaknesses and hide them from the world, this is the area where Christ's strength it best revealed. When we fail to be truthful about our weakness, we refuse Christ an opportunity to speak into our lives and the lives of others. However, when we speak the truth about ourselves or to others, we need to verify that it is being done for the good of the body of Christ—that it will edify or encourage and not inflict harm in any way.

In 2 Corinthians 12:7–10, Christ is revealed as stronger than our weakness. Our weakness then becomes Christ's vessel.

Chapter 5—Sanctuary of Adoption

James 1:17–18. This describes God, our Father, as a giver of good gifts, stable, and unchanging. He personally chose us to be his children "that we might be a kind of firstfruit of all he created." To give us a better idea of what this means, and yet another delightful aspect of God's fatherly love, here is James 1:18 quoted from *The Message:* "He brought us to life using the true Word, showing us off as the crown of all creation." Isn't it just like a good father to show off his children! In what ways do you sense God is proud of you?

Chapter 6—Sanctuary of Compassion

John 11:17–36. In considering Christ's compassion in the story of Mary and Martha, think about and discuss these issues:

His timing

His approach

His words

His actions

His emotions

His purpose and focus

Martha approached her grief by running to meet Jesus as soon as she heard he was coming. She confronted him head on with her grief. She engaged Jesus in a dialogue about her brother and the Resurrection.

Mary handled her grief much differently. She stayed at home. She waited for Jesus' invitation, so he expressed his desire to see her but didn't intrude on her grieving. When she finally met with him, they said very little to each other but shared great emotion.

However we're wired to deal with grief and loss, Jesus is there matching our need to talk, to be quiet, or simply to weep.

Chapter 7—Sanctuary of Peace

The four stories of these people reveal the variety of reasons we feel lonely at times. *The woman at the well* was con-

sidered an outcast for several reasons: She was a Samaritan—
a "half-breed" Jew who faced racial contempt by most
"pure" Jews. For unknown reasons, men had rejected her as
a woman. She was unable to keep one husband. She had been
married five times and now was living with a sixth man. Pos-
sibly this was the reason why she seemed separated from her
community as well. She went to the well at a late hour rather
than with the other women who drew water together in the
early hours. All these reasons no doubt left her in a very
lonely position.

Zacchaeus, a crook by his own admission, had gained his
wealth by extorting taxes from his neighbors. His friends
surely were part of his "network" of collectors hoping to
gain some of the wealth as well. It's hard to imagine that he
had any real, meaningful, intimate relationships. No wonder
he jumped at the chance to welcome Jesus into his home.

Blind Bartimaeus would be an equivalent to the homeless
on our streets today crying out for money or help. Even as
he cried out to Jesus, society seemed intolerant, trying to
quiet his call for help.

John the Baptist, the forerunner for the Messiah, now
found himself in a dungeon, soon to be beheaded by Herod.
How faithfully he had called his countrymen to repentance
and pointed them all toward Christ. But sometimes ministry
is the loneliest place of all. Alone now in a dark, damp prison
cell, he wondered if it was real or just a figment of his imag-
ination. He needed confirmation.

Regardless of the circumstances, all the members of this
"lonely hearts' club" found peace and comfort in knowing
Jesus and in his special message to each one.

Chapter 8—Sanctuary of Faithfulness

God's faithfulness both protects us, like a mother hen protects her chicks, and defends us, like a soldier in battle. Allowing God to be our defense recognizes that we have no defense other than him in the rocky places of life.

Chapter 9—Sanctuary of Deliverance

Discussion about the names of God is covered within the chapter text. Listed below are other names of God and the Scriptures where they're found. You may want to ask each woman to choose one name to study further in Scripture and report back their findings. Or, encourage them to choose one of God's names to meditate on each day.

For a more exhaustive list and study of the names of God, read *Experiencing God: Knowing and Doing the Will of God* by Henry T. Blackaby and Claude V. King.[1]

Creator—Ecclesiastes 12:1

My Rock—Psalm 42:9

God of Peace—Romans 16:20

Almighty—Job 5:17

Lord of Lords—Revelation 19:16

Most High—Psalm 18:13

Majesty—Hebrews 1:3

My Beloved—Matthew 12:18

Chapter 10—Sanctuary of Love

1 Corinthians 13:1–3. Without love, our gifts and service are derived from impure motives. Love must be the guiding force for all our actions.

1 Corinthians 13:4–6. All these aspects of love require a willful choice to obey and let God rule over us. As mentioned in chapter 9, Sanctuary of Deliverance, when we willfully obey, heart obedience will follow. The world and Satan have deceived us into believing that love is a feeling. In fact, Jesus said, "If you love me, you will obey what I command" (John 14:15). Trust him enough to live in this way, and he'll fill you with joy and peace and satisfy your heart's desire for feelings.

1 Corinthians 13:12. Today our sinful nature blurs our vision of God's glory. Even so, his love for us—revealed by the sacrifice of his Son on our behalf—gives us an ability to see more clearly. As we rest in God's sanctuary of love, we begin to extend grace to others. We let go of worry and a need to control when we trust God's lordship and leading. We do not use someone's mistakes as a beating stick. We have no need or desire to puff ourselves up in order to feel good about ourselves. God's love changes how we do life!

NOTES

Introduction
1. Madeleine L'Engle, *Bright Evening Star* (Wheaton, Ill.: Harold Shaw Publishers, 1997), 163.
2. The names of many of the women in the following chapters have been changed to protect their privacy.

Chapter One
1. William Barclay, *The Daily Study Bible Series: The Letters to the Corinthians* (Philadelphia, Pa.: The Westminster Press, 1956).

Chapter Two
1. Tricia McCary Rhodes, *Contemplating the Cross* (Minneapolis, Minn.: Bethany House Publishers, 1998), 76.

Chapter Three
1. Footnote for Hebrews 6:10, *Life Application Bible, New International Version* (Wheaton, Ill.: Tyndale House Publishers; Grand Rapids, Mich.: Zondervan Publishing House, 1991), 2228.

Chapter Seven
1. Chad Larrabee, Canyon Creek Community Church, Chandler, AZ.
2. Emilie Griffin, *Clinging—The Experience of Prayer* (New York: McCracken Press, 1994), 34.

Epilogue
1. Victor Hugo, *The Hunchback of Notre Dame* (New York: Penguin Books, 1965), 362–63, 366–67.

Small Group Notes
1. Henry T. Blackaby and Claude V. King, *Experiencing God: Knowing and Doing the Will of God* (Nashville: Broadman & Holman Publishers, 1994).